BIRTHING ME
MEMOIRS OF A TRANSWOMAN

NAINA MENON

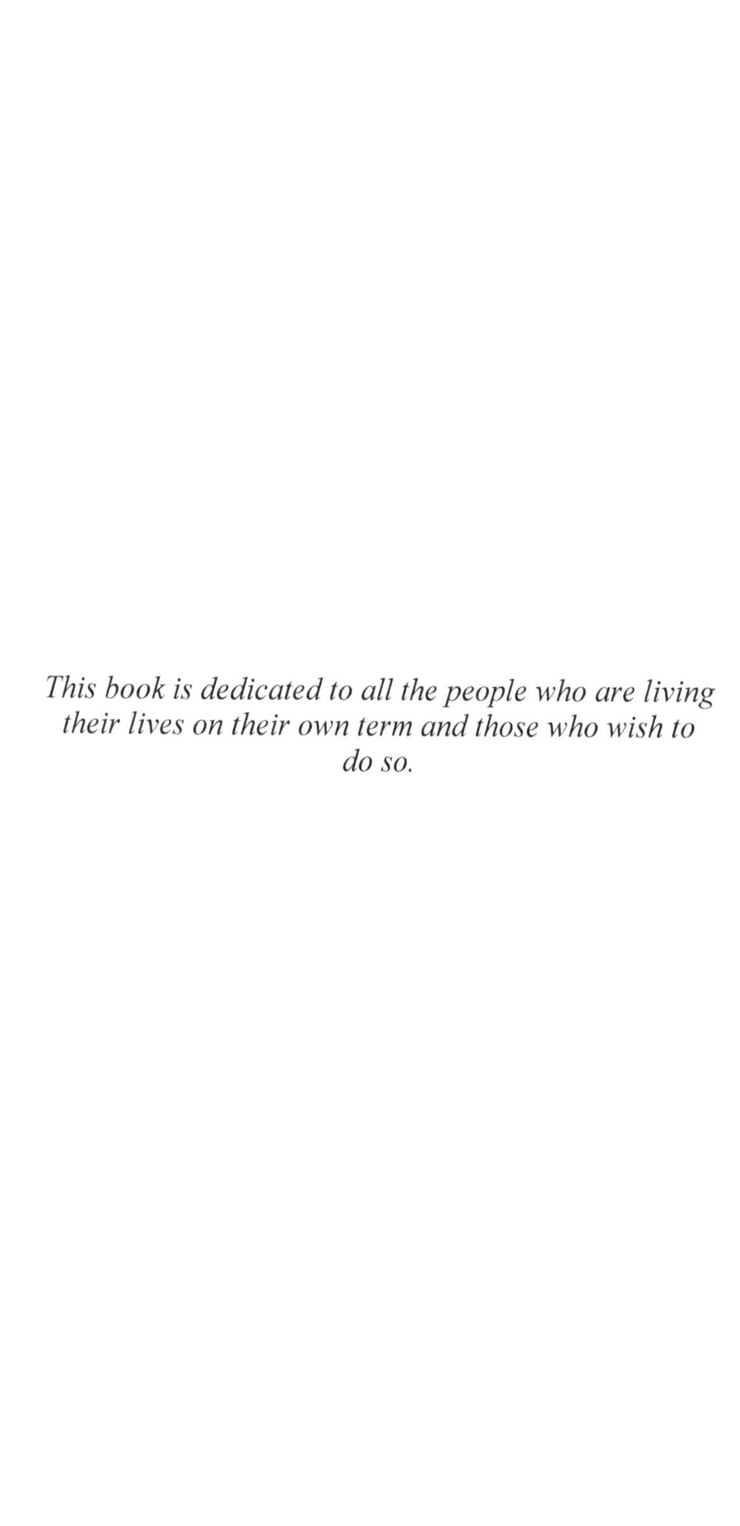

This book is dedicated to all the people who are living their lives on their own term and those who wish to do so.

ACKNOWLEDGEMENTS

Thank you Almighty for bringing light in my life and may you continue to do so. Thank you, dear Guardian Angels who have been constantly looking out for me. Thanking my soulmate Samee for loving me for who I am and bringing love in my life. I thank my parents for giving me this life.

I wish to thank my mentors Shilpa ma'am and Sara ma'am who have constantly motivated me and shown me the light. I thank the beautiful sisters Chechu and Soni who have been with me throughout.

I thank the sisters whom I met by fate, without whom I wouldn't be who I am today – Gurpreet di, Akila & Esha. Thank you for listening to me. I thank Mrs. Rekha Ajay for loving me unconditionally as her own daughter. I thank Archana ma for being there for me always.

I thank Avanti, Shrruti di, Nilshree and all my friends who supported me throughout my journey and still stand tall as my pillars of existence. Thanking Mrs. Mihira Karra for making the wonderful cover page art for me.

I thank the Keshav Suri Foundation for supporting the community in the best way possible and being responsible for bringing a change. I finally thank each and every one, who came into my life and gave me a moment of life and accepted me for who I am.

PREFACE

As the sun's ray emerged from the windows, darkness vanished and the world woke up to chase dreams and fulfil wishes, someone gets up from the bed and stands in front of the mirror. She gazes at her reflection with awe and throws back a smile and a wink , affirming the love that she had for herself. Her dusky body wrapped up in a black silky satin nighty made her feel pretty and confident within the four walls of the house.

She keeps track of time by having a glance at the wall clock and drags herself to the washroom. She again looks at her reflection in the mirror placed above the washbasin in the washroom. She removes the wig from her head and hangs it on the hook on the door. She takes a cotton ball and dips it in makeup remover and starts removing makeup from her face. She then washes her face with a face wash and applies aloe vera gel.

She takes an hour to get ready for the office. Her reflection can't be seen in the mirror anymore. What stands there is a man dressed in shirt and pants having no trace of the woman who stood in front of this mirror a few hours back. Neel puts back Naina's clothes in the almirah and leaves for the office.

LGTBQ+ community is home to millions of people who are in pursuit of living a decent life without the fear of being judged because of social stigma. The people who relate to this community mostly remain in closet. Some find courage, cross the bridge and live life on their terms, while the rest remain locked in a closet. This book will take you through my story of realization, dilemma, struggle and finally finding myself. Every chapter in the book pertains to a particular story in my life which has played a big role in Naina's birth and becoming a woman.

Chapter

ONE

THE TOUCH OF VELVET

The feel of a velvet touch hugging your skin and its softness makes you go mad! That's me. Velvet was once a very royal fabric used by a lot of women for their clothing which saw a decrease in demand over decades. I really don't remember when my affair with velvet began, but I surely know that it's going to stay and blossom throughout this life!

I was a girl in a 10-year-old boy's body, just that I didn't realize this till the age of 23. My father was a government servant, and my mother was a school teacher. I have an elder sister who was ten years older than me, but we never really spent time together because when I grew up, she was mostly away at college and after that got married.

It was the summer of 1998, when I was enjoying my vacation at home. My father was away at the office and my mother had some extra duties of examination paper inspection. I was a very decent and well behaved kid from the very beginning, so I usually didn't get in any mischievous activities in my childhood.

One fine day, I was on the lookout for chocolates that were hidden by my mother. I opened all the almirahs but couldn't find the chocolates. Finally, I decided to open my mother's almirah. I found so many sarees and salwar suits in it. My eyes stopped at one particular cloth. It was jet black and looked shiny. I pulled it out. It was a blouse! It was my mother's blouse that she used to wear with a saree, a velvet blouse! It looked so royal, and I was absolutely mesmerized by its beauty.

I kept looking at it for minutes after which I finally took it in front of the mirror and saw myself holding it. I don't remember what went inside me that day. I kept it back and returned to playing games on my computer.

Days passed by and at a party I saw one of my aunties wearing the same velvet fabric blouse and a matching saree. I loved the way it looked on her. I went back in time when I was holding the same type of blouse at home.

The next morning when no one was at home, I opened the almirah and pulled the blouse out. I removed my t shirt and slid the lovely silky blouse on my skin. It was a little loose, since I was a skinny ten-year-old! Nonetheless I loved the feel of it running on my skin. It didn't match the shorts that I was wearing, so pulled out a petticoat and wore it. I looked in the mirror, but still something was missing. I wasn't feeling the way I should have felt. Something was missing. I saw a washed saree left unfolded for ironing on the bed. I just tied saree somehow in a very stupid manner and stood infront of the mirror. There stood a pretty little girl. I took a bindi that lay sticking to the mirror and placed it on my forehead. I looked happy. I met myself for the first time!

My love for velvet fabric continued and I used to try and wear that velvet blouse and saree whenever I was alone at home. Once my mother had taken part in a kitty party drama and she was playing the role of a British lady. She borrowed a beautiful frilly frock from one of her Catholic friends and bought black stockings for the play. I used to see my mom go for practice with the frock folded and kept in a bag. One day I was alone again, and I saw this frock and stockings on the table kept for ironing. I wanted to get into this beautiful orange colored frock. I touched the stockings and it felt like velvet, though not the same. It still called out to me! I undressed and sat down on the bed. I took these stockings and one by one pulled them up my legs. It felt like another skin! The way it hugged me, I felt as if it was made for me.

I then pulled the frock over my head and zipped it up. I stood in front of the mirror, and I saw myself again! This side of me was magical. She was different. Something about her amazed me. I kept meeting her occasionally whenever it was possible.

CHAPTER TWO

THE HOUSEHELP'S BLESSING

My father got transferred to another city and this time it was our hometown Trivandrum! New city, new school, new friends and life went on as usual. I had just entered my teens and the summer holidays were here again! My mother was teaching at a school that was busier than the previous one. She used to leave in the morning at 8 and come back by 4. Our summer holidays didn't match as I was studying at a CBSE school, and she was teaching at an ICSE school. The summer holidays were really boring this time. I used to go for my sports practice in the morning, come back and play computer games. The maid used to come and prepare lunch for me, clean the house, wash the utensils and leave.

One day I opened my mother's box and tried to search for the velvet blouse that I fell in love with a few years back! Previously I couldn't find it in the almirahs, so I had decided to look for it in the box. I couldn't find it in the top layers. I found a grey salwar kameez that my mother had kind of abandoned since it didn't fit her anymore. I pulled it out and wore it. I used to roam around the house dressed up in the grey salwar suit and feeling good about it. After a few times that I wore it, I felt something amiss. I didn't have breasts! It made me a little sad. I took my mother's bra and wore it.

The toughest part was to hook it up from behind which I mastered in my later years. I stuffed the bra with a few crumpled socks and wore the kameez. Now I went back in front of the mirror and gazed at the girl that was growing up in me. She looked cute and happy! I took the dupatta or the stole and covered my fake breasts with them, just the way girls do! I used to meet this girl every day for about an hour, after which I had to change because the maid used to be home by then.

One day I got dressed and started looking for the velvet blouse again. I pulled out the clothes one by one and kept them on the floor just the way they were put in the box. After about an hour's hard work, I found the velvet blouse and managed to put everything back in the box as it was. Suddenly the bell rang, and my heart skipped a beat. I rushed to the door to see who it was. It was Reshma didi, our maid! I just didn't know what to do. She kept ringing the bell. I opened the door and quickly ran into my room to change. I changed and hid the clothes.

I went to Reshma didi and asked her how she was. I also asked her if she had seen me when I opened the door. She said she didn't and asked me what happened. I told her that I could tell her if she promised me to keep it a secret. She nodded with a smile, and I went inside to change. I got back into the same grey salwar suit, but this time I added lipstick to my look! This was something new, but the lipstick lying on the makeup table just pulled me towards it. I didn't know the correct way of wearing it, but I had seen my mother applying it to her lips and tv icons using it on tv! I got ready and thought for the last time if this was a good idea or not. I stood at the door for about ten minutes and finally decided to go ahead. I walked like a teenage girl to the kitchen and called out her name! She turned back and smiled at me! It was a smile and not a laugh! I still remember, she admired me that day and did not laugh or mock me! We became friends!

She was kind of a replacement for my sister who had always been away from me! 'Chechi', my sister, as I lovingly call her, took an important place in my life quite late. So, every day I used to dress up and wait for Reshmi didi to come home. I used to walk around with her while she worked. We even ate lunch together. I used to change back to my boy clothes when she left for the day. One fine day I asked her if she could drape a saree on me. She happily agreed and asked me to bring a saree.

I ran into the room and pulled out my mother's yellow saree from the box. I wore the velvet blouse and a black petticoat and took the saree to her. She started draping it on me. I couldn't stop smiling the whole time! It was done in five minutes. The pallu fixing required a pin. She pulled out a pin from her saree, just like an elder sister or a mother and fixed the pallu to my shoulder. She took two steps back, came closer and adjusted my pleats. She looked at me, smiled, kissed my forehead and said that I looked like a beautiful little girl! I couldn't help but blush! She took me to the mirror, and we looked at our reflections and smiled!

Reshmi didi served our house for about a year. After the summer holidays, I used to have two hours to dress up before my mother came home. One day Reshmi didi was wearing a velvet blouse that looked prettier than my mother's black velvet blouse. Probably I got bored with the black one! The one that Reshmi didi was wearing, flaunted a beautiful embroidery and had a different feel about it as it was something that I saw for the first time. She saw me admiring it and asked me if I wanted to try that blouse.

I said yes but brought out practical difficulties of how she would get it the next day and which saree would suit it. I went back in the room to watch tv and started thinking if there were any sarees in my mother's box that would go well with that blouse. Meanwhile, Reshmi didi went to wash the clothes. Five minutes later, didi came to me with the blouse and saree!

I had completely forgotten that she used to change into a nighty to wash the clothes in the bathroom! She quickly draped me in the saree and pinned me up. She smiled at me and said that it suited me. She asked me to enjoy myself and watch tv while she could wash the clothes. I instead chose to sit outside the bathroom and talk to her while she washed the clothes. We talked about movies, movie stars, places to visit in Kerala and so much. As soon as she finished washing the clothes and hung them up for drying, I asked her to remove the pin so that I could return the saree and she could change into it. She said, "Girl enjoy for a little while more, I will finish the kitchen work and then change". She changed her routine of changing her saree before the kitchen chores to make me happy!

She kept doing these little things for me occasionally, which meant a lot to me! She even bought a velvet blouse for me from the local market which had beautiful embroidery on it. She left us before the next summer holidays to join her husband in Kuwait. I didn't hear from her after that, except for a phone call where we could talk just for about a minute. Thankfully my parents were not home, and I could express the real me on the phone! I just hope she is happy wherever she is. She filled in the place of my elder sister and gave me unconditional love without judging me. I owe a lot to her.

CHAPTER THREE

HINT TO FOLKS

Senior Secondary School was fast. Time ran like winds and now when I look back, it feels as if it got over in a flash. Physics and Mathematics in class eleventh were a new world order which didn't have any connection to their syllabus in tenth. Every second science student was preparing for IIT and the remaining like me either had no interest in IIT or knew that IIT was not my cup of tea! I was a popular boy in the school since I was good at all the sports and extra-curricular events. I was also the House Captain because of which I had a lot of friends in the junior classes. I was enjoying this popularity and attention.

Away from school, I always missed and remembered the days with Reshma didi. We had shifted to a new housing colony, and we had a different maid with whom I didn't feel like sharing the girly side. I had also started attending tuitions for Math and Chemistry for my twelfth-class board exams. I was never the one who liked sitting in one place, but strangely I loved computers. Online chatting and cyber cafes were in during the year 2005. I loved chatting online as the other person didn't know who you were. One could portray a fake identity, and no one could make out unless they saw you on web cam or talked to you. I used to bunk my tuition classes once in three days and indulge in online chatting. I had made a yahoo mail id by the name of Vandana and chatted with a lot of men, much elder to me as the crowd was mostly college pass outs who were around 6-7 years elder to me. I had a few permanent chat friends who believed in the fact that I was a girl. It was a getaway from studies and refreshed me.

The velvet blouse was a very common thing and I had lived the dream of looking pretty in it. I developed a love for velvet salwar kameez! I kept saving my pocket money and saved money for my bus travel for tuition. Within two months I saved about Rs.600 for the salwar kameez.

The search for a velvet salwar kameez had begun. It was getting out of fashion as it stayed for about three years and fashion was changing fast as India was booming thanks to the IT sector. It was tough to find a velvet suit. I somehow managed to find one at a shop while bunking my tuition classes. I bought it but could make out that it was way too loose for me. I looked for a tailor shop where only a limited number of people were sitting, preferably only one.

After great difficulties, I found a ladies tailor who took my measurements and altered the suit. The reason given to her was that I had a school play and seeing my mixed physique of something like an athletic teenage girl, she was convinced. I took back the suit and was excited to try it out. I hid it in the storeroom of our house that was outside the house. Our house was on the third floor and there were four houses on each floor of the six storied building. The date with the new dress had to wait since the night had crawled in.

The next day I came back from school and rushed to the storeroom to pick up the dress. I pulled out an old bra from my mother's closet and quickly dressed up. I looked in the mirror and couldn't be happier! I changed and kept all the stuff in an old handbag that was no longer used by my mother and hid it in the storeroom.

These dates with the dress continued for a few months secretly. My board exams had started and most of the time I was either studying or playing. I used to find time for the dress once every few days. One day my parents had gone out for a party and I decided that it was a good chance to dress up and stroll on the roof of the building where no one came after sunset. I went to the storeroom and changed in darkness, covered my head with the stole and came out. Suddenly the storeroom of the next house that was opposite us opened up and out came their local help, a young girl in her early twenties who was usually friendly with me. She smiled and was literally in amazement. I told her that I was going to a fancy dress competition. She said she could help me a bit with the makeup, and I happily agreed. I said goodbye to her and enjoyed my time alone at the rooftop for good about half an hour. I thought that she might be someone who could fill in Reshma didi's shoes and I could have a sister!

The next time that I dressed up, it was already dark and I waited in the store room for her to come. After an hour I could hear her footsteps and I walked out to show myself.

She was furious as to why I was doing it again and even threatened me that this would be informed to my mother. I begged her not to and promised her that I would never repeat this. All this happened during my board exams! Now when I look back, I feel I was fearless as I always did what made me happy! I feel proud of it. This chapter didn't end here. The next day in the afternoon, the doorbell rang and I went to open the door.

I saw the same girl standing at my doorstep and with my eyes wide open staring at me fiercely. I saw the bag with my stuff in her hand. She was about to tell my folks about this! She did that and brought along a series of volcanic eruptions with tsunamis at home. My parents gave me a mouthful but brushed it off as something not serious. This happened when my Class 12th Board exams were going on. I can't even imagine now when I see back as to what all I went through. I was confused, hurt and felt lonely.

I had no one to share these feelings that troubled me. Had my parents been aware of the terms that are commonly used today related to the LGBTQ+ community, they would have probably tackled the situation in a much better way. I can't blame them for the generation they were born in or the sermons they got during their upbringing. Right and wrong were clearly defined and there was nothing called "looking at something from a different perspective". Everything was textbook and if it said something was wrong, then it had to be wrong. Society had a major role to play in our lives then.

It was just a few years passed from the Millennium Year and my parents were hugely affected by "what would people say" syndrome. My parents had caught me with women's clothing and wig in my luggage during college days too.

Me and my father had tried talking about it, but those days being trans or being queer was there in no dictionary. Things didn't get any better. I survived my school and college hiding things from my parents, shutting down myself-the real me in a closet which eventually came out at a later stage that proved otherwise ugly for the family. Fireworks were expected considering the conservative middle-class background that I came from.

The only thing that helped me survive through all the struggle was my educational background and the will to live my life on my own terms. As it is said, time heals, and it did. Slowly but gradually my parents were over it is thinking that I had grown over it. But had I? Things were just beginning to cross the State Highways into the National Highways and Expressways! There were much bigger things in store for me and my family ahead.

CHAPTER FOUR

THE FAKE SKIT

I had joined a good college at Bangalore to pursue my bachelor's in engineering. Everything was new for me, starting from staying away from home to staying with unknown people. I never really wanted to be an engineer and would have been happier doing something in the Arts. It's just that I was decent in studies and could crack the entrance exams for engineering that landed me a seat in Bangalore. The college hostel was divided into two wings and we had one wing for the boys and the other for the girls.

It had been quite some time since I had last met the girl in me and now being in the hostel brought further obstacles. I wasn't happy being with the boys, kind of made me uncomfortable. I understood the reason at a later stage in life, but at that moment it was strange for me. The only getaway for me was the weekend visit to my aunt who stayed with her husband and a seven-year-old daughter. They were family friends and had promised my parents that they would look after me. I enjoyed having delicious meals at their place during weekends. My college was around 15 km from the hostel, some reasons due to which the college placed the hostel away from its premises till a few years. Due to the distance and the travel, I usually felt that it would have been better if I had a two-wheeler. I started bunking classes, a lot of them because I was never comfortable in my head. I felt I was with the wrong people around and I started feeling probably I was in the wrong body as well.

College life wasn't treating me so well. I was decent in studies, and I was putting in enough effort to do well in academics, but I wasn't calm and started feeling that something was wrong in my life. I had everything what a college student looks forward to having, at least more than what my parents could provide me. I made a lot of new friends from my batch in college, mostly girls. I always had more girls than boys as friends, because I felt comfortable talking to girls.

I used to secretly admire their beauty and at times used to wonder if I could look like them. Colorful dresses, make-up, beautiful long tresses, really made me wonder why I couldn't have all of these!

Slowly but strongly, I started realizing the girl in me more clearly, because of which I remained disturbed. I wondered why I wasn't born a girl and if this life was a punishment. I loved the way, girls had more choice of clothes, hairstyles and the level from ethnicity to western wear were like two poles where both were within reach for every girl.

One fine day I visited my guardian Priya auntie's house on a working day as I didn't feel like going back to the hostel fearing my seniors and the ragging! Aunty was happy seeing me. She made delicious paranthas for me as I sat and watched TV.

When she finished her chores, she joined me to watch TV. I told her a story that I had made up. I told her that I was selected for a college drama wherein I had to play the role of a girl and I had to go to a senior's house to try out a dress. Unexpectedly, she asked me to stay and promised me that she would arrange a dress for me. I told her specifically that I needed a velvet salwar kameez. She made a few calls on the mobile phone and asked me to come with her to the neighbor's house around 1 km away.

Geeta aunty received us with a smile and when she got to know that the suit was for me, she was so excited! They brought out a green-colored velvet salwar kameez and asked me to try it out. As she walked out of the room with a green salwar kameez in her hand, my eyes twinkled! I was mesmerized by the beauty of the dress even though it would have been a simple piece of clothing for any woman if asked of. I took it in my hands and walked into the bedroom for a trial.

I didn't want to wear my lingerie underneath as it may seem awkward for the women sitting in the next room. I just tried the dress and went out to show myself to auntie. It proved to be quite loose for me, and I wanted it to be body hugging as if it was stitched for me. Geeta aunty knew stitching and used her sewing machine to alter the dress to my fit. I tried the suit after the fitting, and it was so pretty!

Now I decided to put on my lingerie and the wig too! I came out of the room to show them and both aunties adored me saying that I looked like a thin girl. I also had grown my hair long enough to look like a bob cut girl when combed in a particular manner. But I preferred wearing my wig as it gave me the freedom of playing with longer hair! I don't know why but they kept on appreciating my figure as if they knew that I was enjoying it!

After a few minutes, when I was going inside to change, Priya aunty stopped me saying that I can change back at her place. She pulled my leg by saying that it would be fun taking back a pretty girl to her kitchen! So, I pulled the dupatta on my head, and we walked back to Priya auntie's house. I kind of didn't like changing so soon. It was around 10 in the morning, and we had around 3 hours before uncle would return home.

I asked aunty if I could keep wearing the dress for some time as I wanted to get in the role of a girl. She gave me a smirk but played along and somehow, she treated me like a girl as if she knew deep inside that I had the soul of a girl. I helped her chop vegetables and cook too. After about an hour the doorbell rang, and I was a bit scared thinking who it could be. Aunty asked me to relax and went to check.

As I was sitting on the chair and watching TV, I saw two young girls probably two years younger to me enter the room. They joined hands together and respectfully greeted me with "Namaste Didi"! This was probably the first time a stranger had seen me as a girl, and they took me for a girl even without makeup! They had come for collecting a tiffin from Priya aunty. They asked me where I was from and who I was. Before I could answer and spill out the beans, Priya aunty replied that I was Shilpa, a family friend and was visiting her. Once they left, Priya aunty came back in and started laughing thinking about what happened. I liked the name Shilpa, and it was probably my first girl name.

This was just the start and I brought up the college drama idea two more times and tried out a few more outfits. Priya aunty had taken me to cosmetic shops to buy bangles and cheap jewelry for me. She also introduced me to lipsticks and kajal, very simple make up which just accentuated my facial features. It was a great learning, but I had to stop somewhere to draw a line. She had promised me that my girly part won't be shared with my parents, and she kept the promise! I lost touch with her in my second year of college when their family moved to Lucknow. Neither did I, nor my folks know that this phase of my life was going to unleash the real me.

CHAPTER

FIVE

THE FIRST OUTING

When I was in my class 12, I was sent for tuition for Mathematics. Occasionally I used to bunk my tuition classes and go to the Gaming Arcade or the Cyber Café to chill out. Many a time it had occurred to me that why can't I bring my clothes to the Cyber Café, dress up femme inside the closed cubicle and just walk out or maybe change my clothes at an abandoned place. My folks had a Kinetic Honda scooter which mostly lay unused since the time we got a four wheeler. I also had thoughts of dressing up femme and driving the scooter in the city after sunset. Such thoughts kept creeping through my head. I wished to be seen as a girl.

I longed to be adored as a girl but only by unknown people. One day I decided to find an abandoned place to change my clothes. I was able to find a place under construction just above the Cyber Café. It fitted the bill of not being too far from the Cyber Café, being close to the auto rickshaw stand to provide me with a source of public transport and it also lay abandoned since the construction was stalled due to some reason which I never knew. Then I started planning. I mapped the whole plan which included the time to change into my femme avatar, time to start walking towards the destination, time needed to catch an auto rickshaw if need be, time needed to return back to changing place and the time needed to reach the changing place through a different route if someone followed me.

I kept in mind the various situations that could occur. What would I do if someone created an issue publicly? What would I do if some men try to grab me? What would I do if I was not able to change in privacy? So many questions, so many answers. I ensured that I had a plan for everything. I worked it up in detail. The next day I packed my salwar kameez, lingerie, sandals, a ladies handbag and an extra dupatta.

I reached the Cyber Café and got into my cubicle. I closed the door and got dressed up and wore my boy clothes over it. I had decided to do the main change in the Cyber Café and the superficial change along with some make up at the ongoing construction floor above. I checked out of the Cyber Café and checked the surroundings. When I felt safe, I climbed the stairway to the changing place. I got rid of my boy clothes and quickly did some amateur make up which included lipstick and kajal only. I covered my head with the additional dupatta that I was carrying, took the handbag and was all set to leave. I hid my boy clothes and shoes under the construction material that was lying there. I took the step and carefully walked down the stairs. My heart was beating faster than ever, and I was so freaking scared that someone would see me coming downstairs. Thankfully, I went unseen till the road! I started walking and within minutes I realized how hot the weather was. The salwar kameez was velvet and it was body hugging and left me drenched in sweat completely thanks to the humidity of Trivandrum.

I could feel eyes staring at me, some even stopped to have a glance at me. Although I was thin, the covering of my head really left some doubts in the minds of the people who got to look at me. I stuck to the plan and kept walking till the end of the road. I felt thirsty and I had to make amends for my so-called well-revised plan! I found a juice shop which had only one member staff and one customer. I walked up to the juice shop.

Me: One orange juice please.

The shopkeeper looked at me as if he was trying to decipher something from a code that was thrown at him!

Shopkeeper: Ice or without Ice

Me: Ice….

I couldn't utter another word. As I waited for the orange to be peeled and put in a juicer, I wondered how the shopkeeper prepared everything in a jiffy when I went as a guy! Those five minutes felt like eternity. I waited and waited and so many thoughts lingered in my head. I was just thinking about getting back to the changing place safely and heading back home. What if I didn't make it back? What if the cops caught me and took me to jail? I was sure it wasn't a crime, but it didn't confide to what the society saw as Normal.

Shopkeeper: Orange juice with ice.

I took the glass and gulped it down at one go without even waiting to give some response time to my taste buds. Even before my brain could say "wow what a tasty juice", I had finished the whole glass.

Shopkeeper: Rs.10

I just had a note of twenty apart from the hundred that I was carrying. I kept the twenty on the shop desk and started walking back to my changing place. The walk back was scary and exciting at the same time.

By God's grace I didn't find anyone at the entry to my changing place. I changed into my boy clothes, washed my face, checked for any make up traces through a small hand mirror and headed back home.

The excitement of the first outing had finally subsided. I could see how risky and foolish it was to change clothes in an unknown place and walk in a vulnerable state. I must thank my stars that nothing untoward happened and I returned home safely. This outing gave me the strength in later years of my life when I took bigger steps. So, I feel that I was destined to do this!

CHAPTER SIX

THE VIRTUAL WORLD

It was the year 2005. The Internet was booming, and it was accessible to even the lower classes at economical rates at Cyber Cafés. We as college students didn't have fancy mobile phones like the times of today and didn't have access to the world on them. Cyber Cafes proved to be the perfect getaways for email love letters, virtual dating, chat rooms and what not! The mobile phone operators also tried to help by giving us hundreds of free SMS daily packages, which was a big boon. Thanks to the internet, messenger and chat rooms, I was able to create a virtual world where I was a girl. Yes, even I have done such kind of things.

I still wasn't sure as to why I loved to dress up as a woman. I had no clue as to why this thing stuck to me so badly. The only thing I knew was that, dressing up as a woman never made me a bad person, whereas it always helped me gain sanity and composure. I felt empowered whenever I was dressed in women's clothing. I could think better and even stay focused. Shutting this part of me in the closet and hiding it from the world was tough and painful. This is where the virtual world helped me. I was a woman in front of at least about twenty people. I used to log into chat rooms as a woman and chat with total strangers. It was never a sexual desire, but for acceptance as a woman. for which I created the virtual world for myself.

I remember interacting with many decent men, who were looking for something more than just being friends from my female avatar. After chatting for a few weeks with these men, when I started trusting them a bit, I even shared my mobile phone number with them. Yes, I was one of the lucky kids to have a basic phone with me during my senior days at school. I used to call my female avatar as Vandana. There was this guy named Rakesh who seemed to be very nice, and I never thought that he would hurt me. He was honest with me about his work, background and life completely, whereas I wasn't the same with him.

I had created a whole new world for Vandana probably to attract someone towards me to gain all their attention and to feel like a woman. I could modulate my voice, very close to being a feminine voice but I was never confident of speaking to Rakesh on phone. I had warned him that I had a very bad voice, even before we started talking. Whenever we were not chatting, we used to exchange emails. One fine day after a lot of hiccups, I decided to talk to Rakesh on the phone. I dialed his number.

Rakesh: Hello.

Me: Hi Rakesh!
Rakesh: Vandana?

Me: How did you know it's me?

Rakesh: You gave me your number last week but I was waiting for you to allow me to call you.

Me: I am sorry I took some time to call you.

Rakesh: No, it's perfectly fine. I am happy that you connected finally with me on phone. You have a lovely voice and you kept telling me otherwise!

Me: No Rakesh, I have a pathetic voice!

Rakesh: I beg to differ Vandana.

So, this started my virtual relationship with Rakesh which lasted probably for about a year after which he got married to a nice girl. I was more like a close friend to Rakesh. We remained in touch even after he got married. Rakesh was the reason why I learnt a lot of things about being a girl. I learnt how to talk like a girl, how to talk to boys, what is the uncomfortable line for a girl which a boy should never cross. I could see life from a girl's perspective the time that I spoke to Rakesh. It was as if for that period, I was taken into some different world where I was a girl.

There were a few others too with whom I interacted on phone, but none like Rakesh because he was trustworthy. I couldn't trust others as they were never honest with me. I can't blame them, since I wasn't honest with them too! All this started in the final year my school and continued till the first yar of college post which I had made a profile for my female version finally. I had clicked some photos of me dressed up as a woman and found many crossdressers on social media, with whom I shared experiences and learnt a lot. I gained access to the crossdressing community in India and realized that there were so many people like me who had no clue about what or who they were.

CHAPTER SEVEN

SEXUALITY & GENDER

Sexuality and Gender are two different things. Most of the people with whom I have interacted in my life, don't know the difference between the two terms. I don't blame them because such things were never taught to them. Neither the school nor the parents tried to teach these to kids of our generation. Gender is something which defines an individual. If an individual relates themselves as a woman, their gender is female and if a person relates to being a man, then their gender is male. Gender has nothing to do with whom they are attracted to sexually. Sexuality or sexual orientation defines whom one is attracted towards.

It may seem confusing to people who have never thought of the difference, but it is what it is. Gender, sexual orientation and sex are not so complicated ideas and don't exist as black and white, as it involves a wide spectrum. The most important thing to realize is that an individual is never defined by their sexuality or gender. You are you and you are awesome, there is no doubt about it. Every individual is unique and different from one another, we are not robots!

You may come across an individual who was assigned as male at birth but felt like a woman and was attracted to women when they grew up. The sex assigned at birth would be male and their gender would be female or transwoman. There are people who aren't attracted to any gender too. So, society needs to understand that the spectrum is wide, and every individual is precious. Gender or sexual orientation is not going to define how the individual will perform at studies or work. Every individual must have freedom of expression. Now a days the threshold of acceptance has grown by bounds. People have learnt to adjust to a seeing a man on Instagram wearing sarees or skirts and still behaving like how a man should behave according to the societal norms.

People often ask me, "When did you realize that you were not normal". This statement is considered derogatory and must not be used. There is nothing abnormal in relating to a gender that defines you. A person is abnormal when they are fixated to the age-old norms that we followed in the society. I am not talking about culture.

Even our culture has shown traces of the LGBTQ+ community in the past. Culture is precious and must be preserved, although it may evolve with time. I included this chapter for those who have no clue about the terms that I mentioned and after reading this I am sure they will indulge in some research on the internet about the terms in question.

I was always in confusion about my gender and attraction to the opposite sex. My attraction towards a girl was restricted to just loving the person as a human being and having no sexual desires which all my male friends had. I must admit that I never even indulged in practiced orgasm or in simple words masturbated.

All my friends watched porn, which I never enjoyed. I never accessed the internet for nude pictures and videos. They never excited me. I never even knew how to masturbate, until I turned 20 years old. I met a guy through social media who was attracted to my cross-dressed side. I happened to meet him a few times when he used to call a few other crossdressers to his home. We used to change into our female attire and have pizzas, watch television and talk a lot about our identities. It was like an organized discussion about us. He had no sexual desire towards us.

He was a practicing doctor and probably curious about what went in our heads. Later, I got to know that he became a psychiatrist and is doing well. That was the place where I got to know how people masturbate. I don't want to dig into deeper facts, but I gained and learnt a lot from these people. They gave me something which I never knew existed in me.

I remember walking away from my friends, while they discussed about women and sexual intercourse. I always felt uncomfortable looking at someone that way. The farthest that I had gone with a girl in college was a kiss and I have no problems in accepting this as a fact.

I am still attracted only to a woman because I felt more connected with women than men. It is nothing against men. It is just my inclination and liking. There are many men, who are attracted to men only. So, people must understand that the likes and desires of an individual is bound to differ from those of another individual. Everyone comes in a unique packaging and people must learn to accept and motivate them to embrace their identity.

CHAPTER EIGHT

WORK LIFE

My college life was finally over, and I had started working. I had moved to Hyderabad. By the time college got over I was placed in four companies through campus placement. It's not that I was an excellent student, but I was offered jobs just because I was an all-rounder. I was blessed with a good education and had studied in schools from different parts of the country, which helped me become someone who could adjust to any environment. I could multitask and was a jack of all trades. Probably that's what the companies look for when they select suitable candidates for their organization. So, I selected the company that suited my requirements the most and it was a well reputed MNC at Hitech City, Hyderabad.

I had chosen a 1-bedroom hall kitchen apartment at Megha Hills which was quite close to my work place. I found the work environment to be extremely friendly and accommodating. After college, I had decided that it was the right time to let go of my crossdressing feelings and move on. However, I didn't know how I could move on from something that was a part of me.

I remained inactive on social media for some time thinking it would be best to stay away from the virtual world that I had created for Naina. I tried to keep myself busy at work. I tried to socialize more with new people, made new friends, travelled to new places and indulged myself in new hobbies likes reading, writing, sketching and cooking.

Even before coming to Hyderabad, I had thrown all my femme stuff roadside thinking that the clothes could be worn by someone who could not afford decent clothing. Those sarees, salwar kameez and skirts must have been taken home by women who would have worn them for years now. I can vouch for it that the blessings showered unknowingly on me by them would have helped me sail through the struggling years till now. Who knows!

I had kept no trace of anything femme with me to push myself to be the man that my family and society wanted to see me as. It was like living a nightmare in which I had to hide my real self and be what someone else had planned for me. I felt trapped. I felt irritated. I used to party a lot with friends happily and go crazy. Everyone felt that I was probably one of the most suitable bachelors around.

No one knew what I was going through. I had lost touch with the virtual friends that I had made, who used to give me solace in distress. It was as if I was made to lie on the bed with my face staring at the ceiling and a drop of water kept falling on my forehead at regular intervals. A total torture!

I excelled in work and passed my probation period of 6 months with flying colors. My family was happy as I was earning a seven figure salary straight out of college way back in 2010, which was a big deal those days. What was going inside me was accessible only to me and I had decided to keep it that way.

I had become a spend thrift and kept buying things which were not needed essentially. Gadgets, clothes, shoes, room decorations, parties and junk food were the entities where I spent huge amounts. I wasn't saving any money at the end of every month. It was only in the middle of the year 2011 when I had decided to chunk out half my salary just for savings. It was a tough decision for me to shell out half my salary every month for savings as I had adopted a lifestyle that required a lot of money. Soon things changed. When I was left with less money to spend, I grew even more frustrated. I was rude to people and got irritated even at the smallest of things. I began losing friends and gradually became a loner. It was almost two years since I had ventured into Naina's world.

The year 2012 brought a lot of changes and happiness. In the month of September, I had been assigned work in Gurugram, erstwhile Gurgaon. It was a month-long assignment and I was being paid slightly higher for this particular work. Gurgaon was a familiar place to me as I used to visit my parents during my college semester breaks. Delhi was adjacent, where I had done four years of schooling from. I had old friends from school in Delhi, a few college mates were also nearby. So, it seemed to be a breath of fresh air for me from the monotonous life at Hyderabad.

The LGBTQ+ community was still in its nascent stage and not being active on social media meant that I had no clue about what was going on in that world. Nonetheless, it was becoming common to see people from third gender in NCR. Although taunted, ridiculed and harassed, people from the community had begun showing their presence in the environment. One fine day, while coming back from office in an auto rickshaw,

I happened to come across a eunuch. She was begging for alms at a red light crossing. She was dressed in a red saree and blouse which was draped in a very skimpy way, which left her cleavage to be exposed to the lustful men around. Her hair was tied neatly into a low bun with flowers accentuating their beauty. Her makeup was loud for any woman to carry for her daily routine, her hips sway as she walked and clapped in joy. She came up to me and looked at me as if she knew what was inside me. I gave her a ten rupee note, she placed her palm on my head and blessed me.

Eunuch: "Khush reh ladki, tujhe upar wala saari khushiyaan de" which meant "stay happy my girl, may the almighty bless you with abundance of happiness"

I was surprised as to why she had called me a girl? How could she peek inside me and know? Did I do something that gave her a hint? These questions kept pondering my head and I finally reached home.

I decided to dive into Naina's world again. Something in me forced to open my profile on social media all over again. I saw my old friends. I was happy to see them living their dreams secretly. A few of them had improved their makeup skills, a few had gone out in the open dressed up as women, some had bought better clothes and some were just content with what they had. I had received hundreds of messages from my friends who were worried about me. Most of them had thought that I had probably left crossdressing for good and was living a happy life. However, that was not the case and it felt good to finally be back to my real world.

In about a week's time I had decided to go shopping for Naina. I went to Ambience Mall, Gurgaon as it was nearby and had everything available under one roof. Pantaloons was a place where no one asked what you wanted and one could select clothes and accessories discreetly to an extent. I bought a few salwar kameez from the label that I always wanted to buy from, footwear, lingerie and some accessories. I even bought a saree and a readymade blouse from Soch.

Getting blouses stitched to my size wasn't an easy task and which is why I bought a readymade blouse for the time being. Eventually I was able to find a tailor for stitching clothes to my size. The next thing was buying a wig. I had googled for wig shops and just to confirm, called them up on phone and booked an appointment at a selected shop at Saket. I returned home with a beautiful long, straight hair wig with bangs in front.

I was pathetic at doing my own make up and choosing the right make up was a tough task for me, especially because I was dark skinned. Almost all make up videos on YouTube in those days were for the fair skinned women which left me with no choice but to use the shades that they used. I looked for local cosmetics shop at Sector-28 market of Gurgaon. Though a bit nervous, I went inside the shop and asked the lady if she could help me with buying make up for me.

Me: I need to buy some make up for myself. I have a skit in my college.

I could pass off as a schoolboy easily, being skinny and having very little facial hair. I had naturally beautiful eyes, eyelashes, eyebrows, cheek bone and forehead.

Lady: This is a foundation, this is a concealer, this is lipstick. Can you ask the person what all she would need, or do you have a list with you?

Me: Didi, it's for me. I have to play the role of a girl in the skit. I need to use makeup.

The lady started smiling and giggling and looked at the other lady who was probably the owner of the shop. The lady owner intervened and offered help. Her name was Shivani, probably in her late 20s, married as the sindoor on her forehead screamingly specified that for her.

Shivani: So, what's your skin type?

Me: I don't know!

Shivani: Is it dry or oily?

Me: Its dry. I have to apply moisturizer regularly, at times multiple times a day.

Shivani: What's going to be your outfit for the skit?

Me: A saree.

Shivani: Do you have a picture of the saree?

Me: Yes, let me show you.

Shivani helped me buy the makeup and select the right shades. Although I realized years later that those shades of foundation and concealer were not the right ones for me. Make up for the dark-skinned women hardly existed those days or maybe I was at the wrong place. I thanked them and went back happily.

It was finally a Friday night when my office team mates and other friends from the city were planning to go out and party. On the other hand, I was waiting to go home and doll up in a saree and spend time listening to music and getting intoxicated! I reached home at about 7 PM. It took me almost an hour to groom myself which included getting rid of my body hair, moisturizing and taking a hot water shower. I did my makeup, got into my lingerie, slid the blouse on and tied the underskirt. I fixed the wig on my head and looked in the mirror. I saw myself after a very long time. I could see myself content.

I draped the saree taking good amount of time to ensure that the pleats were perfect. I pinned the saree pallu to the blouse and the pleats to the underskirt. I wore my silver anklets, put on a necklace and some bangles. I was ready for the evening! I listened to my favorite music, danced, had beer, cooked and chatted with my friends on messenger. It was the perfect evening that had been missing from my life since I left college. I realized what it meant to me. I didn't know wat the future had for me, so I decided to live my life one day at a time and do whatever pleases me. It kept me sane!

The next morning, I woke up in the saree. I changed into a satin nighty and did my chores. It was time for the maid to come and do up the house. I changed back to being a boy and being miserable. I got a call from my boss who was sitting at Hyderabad.

Boss: Hey, I hope I am not bothering you on a Saturday.

Me: No sir! How have you been?

Boss: Oh, we all are good and are missing you here. Sadly, you might have to stay there for a longer time. There's a similar project that needs to be completed in six months and we are collaborating with an NCR based company who would be developing the game for us. You just need to do the quality checks and let us know if it is good to be sent to L.A. So, enjoy NCR for six more months. One piece of good news is that you are getting a raise.

Me: Thank you sir. I am enjoying the work here. I will keep you updated about the progress. Please let me know when I need to start the next project.

Boss: Sending you the information through email soon.

Me: Bye sir.

Boss: Bye. Take care!

So, I was going to be here till that start of 2013! Life was definitely changing, and I was venturing into a new world. Naina's world was continuously evolving. It was as if Naina was born and was in her childhood at the moment. I liked wearing loud colored clothes, as if I wanted to try all the loud clothes that I missed as a girl child! I was lucky to have met a few crossdressers in NCR and even learnt a lot from them. Life at NCR was truly a changing point in my life.

CHAPTER NINE

DIWALI

The month of festivities had already begun. Dussehra, Karwachauth, Dhanteras and Diwali all packed within a short period where families, friends and all those who care gather and celebrate it with pomp and show. Dussehra had gone by quite uneventfully and I was still in double thoughts of opening to the world about my femininity, although a handful of friends knew about it and were happy to have me in their lives. The sad part was that, being a transsexual was still a new world for majority of the citizens of India, hence I was neither invited by any friends nor they agreed to come over to my place for Diwali as the real me still hid in the closet. I was quite unsure of what I was going to do for Diwali in my small one bhk. I wanted to be Naina and spend time that I would remember. I wanted to get tipsy, smoke and listen to Dire Straits, Deep Purple and Madonna.

It was still three days to Diwali and I decided to go out to a pub since it was a weekend if I remember correctly. Suddenly I got a message alert on my mobile and I saw a message on the Delhi LGBT group regarding a party at one of the pubs. I so wanted to be Naina for this party.

Those days I wasn't living the life of a woman. I calculated so much starting from the time left for the party, the attire, the accessories, taxi, getting ready etc. I had been out for a similar party only once before this. So I knew the place and the conditions that I might face. I selected a beautiful golden sequin short bodycon dress.

I am quite tall for a woman being 5 ft 7 in. I still selected a pair of 3-inch pencil heels for my footwear which was used for my photo shoots those days. I dressed up at my place, sneaked out into a taxi and reached the place by 10PM. The party was boring till almost 11 when I decided it was time to go back. I saw two women along with four men enter as a group.

The woman whom I was watching was so confident, happy and beautiful. I felt as if I wanted to be her. I decided I would hang in for a little while. The party was getting better with good music and the dance floor getting opened.

I decided to go to the bar and order Vodka. I was pulled to the floor by someone. I was furious and as I turned back to see who it was, I saw the same lovely girl! She asked me to dance with her, to which I replied saying that I didn't know how to dance. She danced and asked me to follow her. We danced and soon her whole group joined in. I met her friends, and it was nice. One of the guys in the group asked me for my mobile number. Thanks to being a little tipsy, I found it fine to pass the number. So, we all went back home at God knows what time.

A day before Diwali, I had opened up to a few acquaintances about Naina and I really wanted them to meet the real me. Sad but true, I lost those people from my life! They had started avoiding me and the whole group looked at me like I was a freak show!

I was so disappointed that I packed all my stuff related to Naina and decided to get rid of it. I was so disgusted with myself that I cried all night in the company of alcohol and cigarettes. I was intoxicated to such a level that I just threw the bag out of the building. I woke up after a while and searched for the bag. I ran downstairs and found it lying just outside the lift entry. I kept the bag close to my chest and hugged it like I would never let it go. I decided that it was not just a part of me but the real me altogether which I can never let go. I took the bag back to my house and arranged my clothes and stuff neatly in the almirah. I got into my favorite lingerie and slipped a cute nighty on top of it. I went and saw my reflection in the mirror and smiled! I sent a flying kiss back to my reflection, winked and settled down to sleep peacefully.

It was the day of Diwali, and I woke up to a few messages. At one point of time, I even thought of calling unknown people from social media sites to my place and chill, but that was like highly risky, and I wasn't ready to take such risks yet. Still unsure of my plans that night, I was becoming anxious if I would ruin my Diwali. Still, I got ready without checking my mobile and ironed my lovely yellow Saree for the evening. During lunch I happened to see the messages. The first one was - "Hi this is Shailendra, met a few days back at the pub. Wanted to speak to you about something." I relied on saying that he could call me up. So, it was all about an invitation for Diwali eve at Chetna's house. Chetna was the second woman in the group.

I was in a dilemma. What if a group of guys wanted to rape me and were plotting this. Soon Chetna called up and confirmed that they were not rapists! Dressed in a yellow Saree with a velvet blouse and a bouquet of flowers, I was picked up by Shailendra. We reached Chetna's place, and I met so many people who admired me, complimented me and most importantly accepted me! The party went on with so many discussions.

There were a few who didn't know anything about LGBTQ+ community. Even they were happy to have me there. I played music from my mobile phone, cooked a little, danced and played games. I connected my mobile and played some music when the self-proclaimed DJ of the party had disconnected his mobile phone for some reason. My choice of music was loved by everyone in attendance. This side of me had never gotten so much attention and acceptance. I was sitting here dolled up in a saree at someone's house and enjoying a party!

I always used to think that I never got a taste of "A girl's college life". I felt this was maybe a piece of it that I could savor! Whenever I wasn't doing anything at the party, I was just thanking the almighty for giving me that day. This party and the set of friends that I had made, changed not only me but my outlook towards my future too. I could believe in the fact that I could live the life of my dreams and that too on my own terms.

It was way past midnight and it was time for me to go back. I bid goodbye to everyone, hugged Chetna and booked a cab to drop me back. Going back to my apartment was never an easy task. I usually had to change in the cab itself by making an excuse to the driver that I was returning from a theatre performance or fancy dress! So, things weren't easy, and it was never a bed of roses for me. When I decided to do these things, I knew the risks associated with it, but I was ready to face them because this was like a supply of oxygen for me!

It was one of the best Diwali celebrations that I ever had. The other woman from the pub night, Anushka was not seen. She had gone to Kanpur to visit her parents and I did miss her for sure. She was the reason why I was invited to the party. Will tell you her story soon. She is still a close friend to me and is like a loving sister. I carried back wonderful memories and friends from that night.

CHAPTER TEN

CHATTARPUR

I was already happy with the extended work at NCR, and I was beginning to live life to the fullest. I was saving enough money and with a raise I was able to buy clothes and accessories for Naina's world. I was engrossed in work throughout the weekdays and weekends used to be my getaway into Naina's world. The only thing that pestered me was that I couldn't go out in the open as Naina. The times when I had to change back to being Neel were painful. Changing into boy clothes, removing the makeup and seeing myself back in short hair hurt me. I would wait for the week to get over and spend time in my virtual world.

I had chatted with many crossdressers and even met a few in NCR. I had opened up to one crossdresser from Delhi about my desire to go out as Naina and roam around Delhi. Anita was a seasoned crossdresser, most likely about a decade older than me. She had been going out dressed up in Delhi and had posted so many pictures on Facebook. She was confident and knew the nuances of going out dressed femme in public. She agreed to have an outing with me. She asked me to bring my clothes and stuff with me to a bus stand close to her house. When we met, I was shocked! She looked totally different from her pictures.

As a man, no one could even have the slightest of doubt about her crossdressing. She took me to a parlor. This was no ordinary parlor. Here, crossdressers came to doll up. Some just spent time there, dressed up and a few went out from there to roam around. This was a new world to me totally! I had never thought that such places existed! The parlor was owned by a makeup artist who was a male to female crossdresser herself. So, a male to female crossdresser is someone who is a man but cross-dresses as a woman whenever they want to. I dressed up in a saree and did my make up. Anita also got ready by the time I did. She wore a simple salwar kameez. I felt a little overdressed for the outing and confessed the same to Anita.

Anita: Why are you scared? It's your life, your wish. You are not committing a crime. You are just living your life and going out sightseeing just like any other human being would do.

Me: But am I not a bit overdressed? I totally look like a guy in a saree.

Anita: Who said so? Trust me, the figure that you have, many girls would die to have that! Yes you need to work on your face and make up but your gestures and mannerisms are totally femme. Covering the face, no one can make out that you are a guy. Even your face is quite thin and feature rich, so you do look feminine. Just work a little on the makeup part next time.

I was satisfied with what she said and gained some confidence. We went out, walked about a kilometer to the main road and hired an auto rickshaw. We reached Chattarpur. There was a temple and a park where a lot of crowd had come. We first went to the park, clicked pictures, walked around ignoring the stares that we got from people. Initially it was a bit of an uncomfortable experience for me as people stared at me an tried to analyze who I was. It was not just men but women too who looked at me in an unwelcoming manner, but I was determined to enjoy my outing. This was my first proper outing as Naina.

CHAPTER ELEVEN

THE LOVE FOR NCR

Gurgaon and Delhi always had a special place in my heart. These cities gave me the freedom to go out in the open without fear. No matter how many crimes have taken place here, I may have been lucky or blessed enough to have walked through these cities in my portals of time, safe and sound. These cities have nurtured me over time and gave me the strength to face the world on my own.

There is a different connection that I have always felt with Delhi. A city which was destroyed and built seven times, a city which has preserved in its soil, the composite culture of thousands of years and which has adopted anyone and everyone who has come to its land in search of opportunity and a new life.

The soul of Delhi is recognized only by a small set of people like me who can relate themselves with Delhi and find a connection among the hidden ruins, the streets, the traffic and the people. I have had the opportunity of studying in Delhi during school and also kept coming back to the city during my semester breaks in college. The city has definitely given me much more than I can ever offer back to it.

I had already calmed my worried mind by gifting myself an outing that was etched in my memory forever in golden letters. We were into the year 2013 and my extended project seemed to have stretched longer than the scheduled timeline.

Even the Head Office at Hyderabad had agreed to place me in Delhi for a longer time and they had no qualms about it since it was an important project for the future. So, I was adopted by Delhi with open arms and I kissed Delhi back for giving me all that I wanted. I kept calling out my real self Naina out on weekends where I was left to enjoy.

Work was smooth, finances were strong, health was at its peak and happiness had no limits! Still, there was something missing. I felt lonely occasionally. Whenever I went out with my friends in my boy mode, I admired the women who walked freely clad in sarees, salwar kameez or western attires. I noticed their hair, their makeup, their gestures and mannerisms and practiced them at home. It didn't come easy for me.

I never showed signs of being effeminate throughout my school and college. I had always tried to hide the real feelings and replaced them with fake male mannerisms. Delhi gave me the freedom to explore and bring out the feminine side of me that was buried deep inside me.

I always looked at the eunuchs and felt the sense of liberty that they had to dress up the way they wanted to. Although I agree, the suffering and prejudice that they go through is something which is not everyone's cup of tea. We can't even imagine what sort of life they live and what kind of torture they go through to feed themselves and live. I had a desire in mind to walk freely like a eunuch on the streets of Gurgaon, especially the MG Road area which is a home to multiple Malls in the city.

I decided that I could probably book a hotel room, change to Naina and hit MG Road. I had never done this at a hotel. I called up a few hotels and told them that I had to change as a woman for a skit and go from the hotel. I had also informed that I would be coming back the same night and be checking out the next morning. Although a few hotels agreed, I wasn't comfortable with the way they spoke. One hotel seemed decent, and I zeroed on to it. I packed my stuff, took a cab and reached the hotel. As I was checking into the hotel, the receptionist asked me.

Receptionist: What time would you be leaving for your program?

Me: 8 PM.

Receptionist: Any cab or auto needed?

Me: Yes, I would like to have an auto rickshaw called for.

Receptionist: Please let us know whenever you are ready. I will call for an auto rickshaw.

Me: Thank you.

Receptionist: Which place should the rickshaw be booked for?

Me: MG Road.

Receptionist: Ok.

Me: Bhaiya, I hope there is no issue in me changing into a woman and leaving from here.

Receptionist: Please don't worry, this place is absolutely safe.

Me: Thank you so much.

I was checked into my room soon. I took a shower and got dolled up in a black georgette saree with a full sleeves silver blouse. I looked loud for sure, but that's what I wanted to feel and see out there. I left my hair open and smoked a few cigarettes. I had butterflies in my stomach. I couldn't decide whether to go out or not. It was already 7:30 PM and according to my plan I had to leave by 8 PM. I decided to order a cold drink and spend some more time in the room. As the hotel boy rang the bell, I was a bit jittery while opening the door. Even he was a little surprised seeing me in that avatar. He gave me a smile when he left the room. I thanked him while he walked away taking the payment for the cold drink. I called up the reception at 8 PM and requested an auto rickshaw.

In about ten minutes I got a call back and was informed that the auto rickshaw was at the hotel gate for pick up. I sprayed my whole body with the most girly deodorant that I could pick up from the market. It was canned in a baby pink color too! I fragrance made me feel more feminine and confident. I took my handbag, pinned my pallu to the blouse and walked out confidently. As I reached the reception, a few men glanced at me. Ignoring them, I spoke to the receptionist, thanked him and boarded the auto rickshaw.

Driver: Where do you want to go?

Me: Bhaiyya, please take me to MG Road.

Driver: Rs.50

Me: Ok, that's fine with me.

The driver kept glancing at me through his rear view mirror. Meanwhile I kept adjusting my pallu, ensuring that it covered the front part of my blouse well. I was dropped a little ahead of Sahara Mall at MG Road. I kept walking on the opposite direction from Sahara Mall as I didn't want to jump into the crowd straight away. I had even noticed a few cops in front of the mall and wanted to avoid them at all costs. Although, I wasn't here to do anything illegal but I didn't have answers to the questions that would be put forth if confronted.

I walked up to a Paan shop and asked for a cigarette and a 'meetha paan'. I then walked up to the nearest metro station , looked around and came out. I didn't know what to do. I just wanted some attention from strangers. I was prepared to get a lot of stares and was also ready to be laughed upon at. I caught an auto rickshaw to go back to the hotel room. Finally when I reached the hotel, the receptionist gave me a warm smile and I sneaked into my room. I remained in the attire for the whole night, got drunk and slept! This concluded my second outing in Delhi and that too solo!

CHAPTER TWELVE

THE FIRST PHOTOSHOOT

It was the end of 2013 when I got a chance to get my first photoshoot done! I wasn't ready for a full-fledged photoshoot that pertains to a portfolio for modelling. I wasn't ready to spend huge amounts for this sake. I searched for budget photographers on google and selected a few with whom I could discuss my needs.

Photographer: Hello.

Me: Hi, I need to get a photoshoot done from you.

Photographer: Certainly. May I please know what are your requirements?

Me: I am a theatre artist and I mostly do female roles. So, I need to get a photoshoot as a woman.

Photographer: How many outfits and how many photos?

Me: I just need the soft copies of all photos along with some edited ones in which you can do the touch up.

Photographer: No prints required?

Me: No, only soft copies required.

Photographer: Outfits and make up?

Me: I would want two sarees and two western outfits to be covered. I would do my own make up.

Photographer: It would cost you 5000 bucks.

Me: That's fine with me. When can we do this?

Photographer: We can do it this weekend on Friday, if you are ready.

Me: would you have a place for me to change at your studio?

Photographer: Yes, you can change here safely.

Me: Thanks, I will be there by around 7 PM on Friday. Bye.

Photographer: Bye. See you!

Now I had to look for two new sarees, their blouses, some jewelry, new makeup and some attitude for the camera! I went shopping the same evening at Sadar Bazar in Gurgaon. I went into a saree shop. Most of the saree shops were heavily crowded and it was really difficult to get attention when a man goes to a saree shop. I was well versed with the fabrics that were available in the market. I was inclined towards velvet for blouses and georgettes or satins when it came to sarees. The shopkeepers always try selling sarees to their male customers at higher prices, since men have feeble knowledge about sarees. But this shopkeeper didn't know who I was! I was clear about what I wanted to buy, the material, the color and the pricing too! I was able to buy two sarees and matching underskirts from there.

The next step was to get a tailor to stitch the blouses for me. I roamed around the market and nearby places in search of a ladies tailor. I found a few but chickened out from going there as I thought it might be too embarrassing to open up to so many women at the same time in the shop. I was able to find one tailor shop which had only two tailors, both male and just a few customers. I kept circling the shop, waiting for the customers to leave. I even cursed the customers in my head when they were taking too much time just chatting with the head tailor. Once they left, I wasted no time and rushed into the shop, opened up my bag and put the two sarees on the table.

Me: Bhaiyya, I need to get the blouses stitched for these two sarees. The blouse pieces are attached.

Tailor: Measurements?

Me: You can take them now. It's for me, I am taking part in a skit. But I need the blouses ready by Thursday afternoon.

The tailor smiled but didn't make fun of me. He was fine with it as long as he is getting money. This wasn't the first time that I had been to a ladies tailor. Way back in college, I was able to find a lady tailor who was sweet enough to stitch blouses for me. She had even asked me to try them out in the changing room before I took them home. She was a very sweet lady and I remember her fondly. She gave me my first tailored blouse, definitely a big achievement for a crossdresser in those times! So, coming back to the tailor at Sadar Bazar, he took my measurements and even suggested me to go for shorter sleeves which was called Mega Sleeves, a new term for me. I wanted a cute long dori at the back and requested for pads to be placed in the front. He asked me what I wished for neck and back design to which I replied "Very Deep". I still laugh at myself when I think about it.

The blouses were ready by Thursday, and I collected them after the office in the evening. I rushed home just to try them on to see if they fitted me well, and they did for sure! I was very satisfied with the services of this particular tailor who wasn't judgemental and at the same time was extremely professional in his work.

I still get my blouses stitched from him when I am in Gurgaon. I waited desperately for Friday evening. In the meanwhile I had brought the remaining things from my checklist too. On Friday, at the office I kept thinking about the photoshoot. I was so excited. I even searched google for poses that I could replicate in sarees and gowns. Finally, it was time for me to leave the office. I reached home by 5 PM, took a quick shower, packed my stuff and left for the studio. I reached the studio at sharp 7 PM and I met the photographer who was delighted to meet me. His name was Nilesh and had become a professional photographer recently. It was a small studio set up in the near vicinity of Karol Bagh.

Nilesh: Would you like to discuss the photoshoot first and then change or first change into the first outfit and then discuss?

Me: I think let's not waste time and let me change. While I do my make up, we can start discussing.

Nilesh: Yes, that sounds perfect. You can change in this room and once you are ready for discussion, just call me.

Me: Thanks.

I opened the bag, undressed myself and took out the first saree. It was a golden beige saree designed in georgette brasso blend and it shined so beautifully! I draped the saree as quickly as possible, put on my wig and sandals.

I called up Nilesh to discuss the shoot. While I did my makeup, Nilesh showed me different poses on his laptop that I could replicate. We discussed the lighting and the composition of each picture that we were going to click. He also advised me on what style pallu would look good with different compositions. We were set for the first shoot. Initially, I had an inhibition to pose freely in front of Nilesh. I took some time to open and be comfortable. I was giving really weird poses and I thought to myself, I can do better, then why am I not! I took a deep breath and thought to myself, "There isn't a prettier girl than me in this studio. I am as pretty and sexy as any girl would want to be, so pose for the camera an let the lens say Wow". I opened my eyes and swayed my hips to one side, adjusted my pallu, placed one palm on my waist and another rubbing my chin.

Nilesh: Yes! That's the pose, now we are talking!

I blushed and continued with the same attitude. We clicked pictures in this saree for almost half an hour. The remaining three outfits took another two hours. At the end we were done for the day with almost 500 raw pictures, most of which came out beautifully.

Nilesh: I will edit around 100 pictures and the remaining I will deliver in raw format.

Me: When can I collect them?

Nilesh: Give me atleast two days.

Me: Thank you Nilesh, it was fun working with you.

Nilesh: Oh, don't thank me! It was a different experience for me. I must say you were very natural in front of the camera. You were born to make a mark here. Do you mind if I ask you something?

Me: Sure, please ask.

Nilesh: I somehow felt there is a woman inside you. When you gained confidence during the shoot, you were so natural. The poses came so naturally to you. The gestures were just perfect. It's hard to believe that you are a guy! Please don't mind what I said.

I was smiling deep down when a photographer's eyes saw the real me!

Me: No, that is so sweet of you! Thanks a ton for the compliments.

Nilesh: See you in two days!

Me: Bye.

I left the studio after changing, although, I felt like going out as Naina and spending the evening at some good restaurant. I reached home so happy that I was actually shouting and singing songs like a little girl! This was the first photoshoot that gave me the strength and courage to pose confidently infront of a stranger's camera. This was the first step to the pageants and shows that I took part in the future.

CHAPTER THIRTEEN

MUMBAI

The year 2014 brought with it new hopes and challenges for me when I started exploring Naina's world at greater depths that I had never been to! The LGBTQ+ community was gaining more visibility and I got to know about many prominent figures like Dr. Lakshmi Narayan Tripathi, Miss Kalki Subramaniam and many others who have been responsible for spearheading the struggle for the rights of the community. The members of the community who remained closeted slowly started gaining the courage to break the shackles and feel free to express themselves the way they wanted to. The Supreme Court had reinstated Section 377 of the Indian Penal Code, which criminalizes 'unnatural sex'.

The year saw momentum in Pride Parade Marches too, which motivated the community members to stay strong. It gave hope to thousands of people like me who were stuck in the wrong body. I was happy that I wasn't alone. I had always felt that I was one of a kind and my birth was probably a mistake.

I had begun opening to my close friends, which included only women! I was definitely much more comfortable opening up to women than men. I somehow felt that, a man would never be able to understand as to why someone who was born as boy would choose to live the life of a woman. However, a woman would at least try to understand the situation to some extent if not completely and I was almost right about this.

I mostly opened up to a few women from my class in school, at work and some friends that I had made through common friends. Most of them turned out to be extremely supportive and encouraged me to keep going. A few of them even sent me articles of famous transwomen who had started new lives with new enthusiasm! One such friend was Catherine who lived in Mumbai. She was my classmate from school, and we were like buddies back in 2001. I still remember asking her if she could lend me her salwar kameez way back in school! She was so close to me that I was sure that she wouldn't tell this to anyone. Although I hadn't told her the real reason and stuck to a reason that I lost a bet and had to dress up as a girl. We remained friends even after school and kept in touch whenever possible. She had moved to Mumbai in the year 2012 and was after me since then to visit her. I had decided to open up to Catherine and called her up.

Me: Hi Cat!

Cat: Hey Niki! How have you been?

Me: I have been ok ok. Do you have some time? I need to open up to you about something.
Cat: Oho, I have all the time for you. Tell me what's bothering you?

Me: I have a strange habit that has become a part of me and I don't know if it is right in the eyes of society. I am going deep into it and I don't know what the future holds for me.

Cat: Come to the point Niki and as far as society is concerned, as long as you are not killing or hurting someone, it is absolutely fine. Now tell me what it is all about?

Me: I am sending you something on messenger. Please see and then reply.

I sent two photos of me dressed up as a woman to Catherine. I waited for the pictures to be sent. As the circle at the center of the pic turned from transparent to half green and then full green, followed by a double tick, I waited anxiously for Catherine's reply. The tick turned blue, and my heart started beating rapidly. I wondered if I had made a mistake by opening up to her. What if I lose her as a friend? What if she leaks the pictures to my male friends? What if I become the joke of our class? Should I delete the photos now? Should I tell her that it was just a prank and those were edited pictures?

I kept the phone to the side and waited. I was sweating vigorously. I didn't know what to do now! The phone beeped, giving me the signal that a message was received. I opened the lock and saw her reply.

Catherine: Is that you Niki? Wow! You look so pretty! This is amazing, who draped the saree for you?

Me: You didn't find it awkward?

Catherine: Awkward? Why? Surprised- yes! I could have never imagined you as a girl, but I always admired your facial features and wished if I was blessed with them instead of you! So, was this for some fancy dress party?

Me: No Cat, I am a crossdresser or maybe a woman in a man's body. I have been dressing up as a woman secretly since a very long time.

Catherine: So, where's the problem in it? I don't think it's a crime! Even if all your friends ditch you, I am there for you! Don't worry!

By this time I sent her about 20 more pictures of Naina and I was happy to have tasted acceptance from a friend. I had longed for this for a very long time and finally I had a friend from my real life who was there to listen to me, admire me and even guide me! I called her up again as messaging her and waiting for her to reply was increasing the anxiety in me.

Me: Hi Cat.

Catherine: Dude!!! You look so pretty!!!

Me: Please Cat, don't call me a dude! It hurts, especially when you know the real me.

Catherine: Ok, babe! Is that ok?

Me: Better!

Catherine: Who drapes the saree for you?

Me: I drape it myself! I learnt it when I was in school.

Catherine: That is so cool! I can't drape a saree that well! How much time do you take to drape a saree?

Me: About five minutes.

Catherine: Babe, you are going to teach me how to drape a saree. When are you coming to Mumbai? I don't want any excuses, I want you here as soon as possible and you are going to stay with us.

Catherine was in a live in relationship with a man that she had met at work. I had no interaction with her partner, and I had no clue as to how he would react to all this if I stayed with them in Mumbai.

Me: Will your partner be fine with this?

Catherine: Oh, Tupu is a sweetheart! Trust me, he is going to treat you like my sister or maybe his sister. Don't think too much, just come over. We will have so much fun. You can doll up and stay like that all the time. We can cook together, gossip and party!

Me: Next week then! I will be there by Friday and leave by Saturday.

Catherine: Bullshit! Girl, you are coming on Friday, and you will leave only on Monday! I won't let you leave before 10 AM Monday.

Me: Done deal! Let me book my tickets.

Catherine: Don't forget to get your sarees, suits and make-up! I really want to spend time with Naina. Don't you dare chicken out!

Me: Bye Cat! Thanks for everything!

Catherine: Thank you for coming here. Bye!

I booked my tickets from Delhi to Mumbai for Friday and Mumbai to Trivandrum for the following Monday. I was to go home to meet my parents at Trivandrum after meeting Cat. I was so excited about meeting a friend from my real life as Naina. The day had come, and I reached Mumbai with a lot of things to look forward to. It felt like a dream, which I thought would never happen. I reached the address that Cat had given and was received by Cat and Tupu at the entrance of their apartment building. The couple hugged me and Tupu carried my suitcase into the lift and then the house. It felt like he saw me as a woman already! He was chivalrous, friendly and warm. He definitely treated me as his sister-in-law!

Catherine: Tupu, so you finally met my sister!

Tupu: Yes, but I guess I will ask Naina to be my sister! Naina or Niki or Neel? What do I call you?

Me: Anything that you feel is right.

Tupu: Niki?

Me: Now don't make me blush!

Catherine: I don't want to see you in these boy clothes anymore. I hope you got your pjs or nighties. Change into whatever you are comfortable with and then come out. Tupu, go out and get some drinks and snacks. Rest I will order. Come on now, get on to your tasks!

I was guided to their bedroom. It was a one-bedroom apartment and I suddenly wondered where I would sleep. While changing, I decided that I could sleep in the hall where the TV was placed and chill at night watching TV. I changed into a kurti and churidar that I had bought from my favourite brand W. I put on some make up and fixed my wig. I tied my hair into a beautiful braid and covered my chest with a dupatta. I was ready to go out and show myself to Cat. I heard that Tupu was back and I felt a little inhibition in going out of the room. Cat came over and knocked on my door.

Cat: Are you ready my Princess?

Me: Ah, yes!

Cat: Then come out, will you?

Me: Can you come in and see me first Cat?

I unlocked the door and Cat walked into the room. Her eyes were wide open, and she flaunted a wide smile. None of it looked as if she was making fun of me. It definitely seemed as if her feelings were pure and true.

Cat: That's my sassy girl!

She came forward and hugged me! She went to her dressing table and took out a bindi from her drawer. She placed it on my forehead.

Cat: Now that completes your 'shringaar'! Now, step out of the room. Tupu is here and we are eagerly waiting to host you!

I stepped out of the room holding Cat's hand as if a bride was walking into a room! Tupu walked up to me and with a warm smile and gleaming eyes hugged me.

Tupu: Welcome to our home Niki. Feel free to be however you want to be. No one is going to judge you. For us, you are family. Cat and I are delighted to have you with us.

I was teary eyed as he said this.

Cat: Naina, come let's unpack the snacks and get your drink from the refrigerator. I hope you still prefer beer.

Me: Yes, beer would be fine.

We opened up the snacks and transferred the contents on different plates. Tupu had to go to a friend's place to pick up a package urgently. So it was me and Cat left alone to have some girl's time for a few hours. I had longed for such an experience all my life. Here, I was being treated like a girl and it felt as if two long lost girls had reunited and were narrating stories. Cat listened to me with utmost attention and I kept talking as if a pandora's box had been opened up! She didn't shy away from asking me questions that only a girl would ask another girl and this gave me so much satisfaction and assurance of being accepted as Naina. The bell rang and I looked at Cat.

Cat: That must be the burgers that I ordered. Can you collect it?

Me: Are you sure? Wouldn't it look odd? What would the delivery boy think?

Cat: Yes! No need to overthink lady! Go and collect it like a good girl!

Me: Fine!

I shakily opened the wooden door and through the netted door, I could see the delivery boy standing and waiting for me to collect the burgers. I opened the netted door and collected the package.

Me: Bhaiyya, how much?

Delivery Boy: Ma'am, 450.

I took a Rs. 500 note and gave it to the delivery boy. As he was taking out the remaining change to give back to me, I spoke.

Me: Please keep the remaining as a gift and not a tip!

Delivery Boy: Thank you so much ma'am. You are generous! May God bless you!

Me: Good night and thank you!

Delivery Boy: Thank you ma'am.

 I closed the door and joined Cat again.

Cat: How was the experience?

Me: It was something I would have never done, had you not forced me to!

Cat: Babe, you don't know how pretty and graceful you are. Being a woman comes so naturally to you. I am so proud of you, that you embraced the woman inside you.

Me: Thank you for accepting me, Cat! You don't know how much this means to me. I had been craving for such a thing to happen and you gave it to me wrapped in love!

Cat: Oh, cut the crap! What are friends for.

We clicked so many pictures, remembered old times at school, gossiped about the people we knew and watched television. Tupu joined in a few hours and wanted to know what he had missed. Cat narrated the delivery boy experience to Tupu, and he regretted not having been with us during that moment. As we decided to wind up, Cat took me to the bedroom and asked me to sleep there. Cat and Tupu had decided that they would be sleeping in the hall. Even after refusing, they didn't agree and finally I had to move in to the bedroom to sleep. I decided not to change into Neel till the trip was over. I slept as Naina after changing into my nighties. The next morning, I woke up early, freshened up and went to the kitchen. I prepared hot coffee for all of us and woke them up.

Cat: Girl, you made coffee for us? You are ready already? Wow!

Tupu: Cat, learn something from my sister!

Cat: Oh, shut up, she is my sister and not yours!

Me: Stop fighting and enjoy your coffee!

Cat: Do you want to go out clubbing tonight? It's Saturday!

Me: I don't know!

Tupu: We can all stay here and party or maybe watch some good movies on television.

Cat: Done!

That day we had a wonderful breakfast, did the household chores and cooked lunch together. After lunch, we relaxed. I placed my head on Cat's lap while she listened to music on her I-Pod. I don't know when I slept off and woke up in the evening.

Me: Why didn't you wake me up? You kept sitting like this for the whole time?

Cat: I loved seeing my sister sleep! You looked so innocent. It was a delight to watch you!

I blushed! We watched a movie together that night and on Sunday Cat and Tupu had some guests over. They had purposefully called some trustworthy friends to build my confidence. Intentionally they never informed me about this plan of theirs. This was the first time I had faced a group of people as Naina at a house. There is nothing much to narrate about the incident as the set of people who came had the same attitude towards me that Cat and Tupu had. They were all extremely accepting and didn't judge me at all for who I was. The trip was over on Monday and I changed back to Neel to catch a flight to Trivandrum to meet my parents. Changing into Neel was painful. I felt as if I was extracting the soul from my body. I felt embarrassed going out as Neel again. I felt disgusted. I don't have enough words to describe the feeling, which was intense. I still managed to bid goodbye to Cat and Tupu. I thanked them for their love and acceptance   and   left.

CHAPTER FOURTEEN

MALLS DON'T JUDGE

The year 2014 was as it is eventful with the Mumbai trip fresh in my mind. It opened many doors for me. I wanted to go out dressed up as Naina more than ever before. I felt this different level of confidence when I was Naina within the four walls, but I wanted to see if I could replicate the same confidence outside in public too. LGBTQ+ parties and going out with friends was a different thing where I had people from the community around who would never judge me. Going to a place where I had to walk on my own, interact with strangers, being stared upon with unwelcoming looks and still walk with my head held high.

I kept thinking as to which place would be suitable to go as Naina. I first thought of Connaught Place as it was one of my favourite places to be at. I visited CP as Neel just to see it from a different perspective this time and understand the pros and cons of visiting CP as Naina.

I somehow felt that I would be grabbing too much attention to a varied variety of people, all at the same time which was not going to be comfortable for me. I thought of Ambience Mall, Gurgaon as the next suitable option. I took my car and reached Ambience Mall, Gurgaon.

As I walked in the mall through the elevator, I kept an eye on each aspect that I would have to face when I would enter the mall as Naina. The man giving the parking ticket, the security check at the entry of the mall, the elevator man and then the store staff present inside the mall.

I glanced across the three floors of the mall and checked where all I could go. I selected a few clothing stores, gadget stores, jewelry stores and finally a plush fine dining restaurant. I made up a plan and made up my mind that I was going to do this. I decided to wear a long kurti with leggings for this visit, yes of course from my favourite brand W!

The next evening was a weekend and the mall was bound to be flooded with a lot of people. I was still unsure of whether I should go ahead with this plan or not. Friday was a holiday at work and I had the whole day to think about this.

I kept building anxiety in me, thanks to my overthinking antics. Finally I decided to go ahead with the plan as I didn't want to regret the next day not having done it when I had a clear cut opportunity. So, I packed my stuff and drove my car to the hotel.

I parked the car safely and checked into the same hotel in Gurgaon that gave me my outing at MG Road. I checked into the room, took a shower, moisturized my body and got into my salwar kameez. I was getting better at makeup, thanks to the videos that I was watching on YouTube. I did my makeup, fixed the wig to my head and prepared my handbag. Getting out of the hotel wasn't a new thing for me, so I wasn't feeling jittery this time. I locked my room and walked out confidently towards my car. I fixed the seat belt and started the car. I felt that I was looking too tall for a girl while sitting inside the car, so I adjusted the height of the seat in such a way that I appeared short heighted to someone looking at me from outside. I carefully reversed the car, turned on the headlights and the air conditioning.

I started my drive to Ambience Mall, Gurgaon. I realized that this was the first time that I was driving my car as Naina! I dodged through the traffic and took a U-turn to take the exit for entry into the mall. I took the turn and entered the mall premises. My car was second in line to be frisked by security at the vehicle entrance for parking. I reached the check point. I was asked to open the boot of the car. Thankfully my car had the option of opening the boot from inside. It was a comparatively new thing for even a premium compact car like the Polo which I owned. I was asked to enter the parking area. I was given a parking ticket by the parking executive at level 1 basement parking. He didn't give me any doubtful looks, surprisingly! I looked for a decent parking space, preferably close to the elevator, but couldn't find one. I had to park my car around 100 meters from the elevator area.

I took my bag, did some touch ups to my makeup and got off the car. I locked the car and started walking towards the elevator area. I realized that I was walking like a guy. I was wearing flats and it was easier for me to walk like a woman when I was wearing heels. So, I made some corrections in my head and gave my walk some feminine dose. I took smaller steps putting one foot ahead of the other, swaying my hips, leaving one hand free to follow the body and the second hand holding the bag. I also concentrated on keeping my posture right and shoulders upright. Now I felt I was doing it right but I had to constantly keep reminding myself of this time and again.

I was checked by a lady at the security check before entering the elevator. She gave me a warm smile as I left and entered the elevator. A couple entered the elevator with me. The lady, likely to be in her early 20s, definitely unmarried, seemed quite uncomfortable sharing the elevator with me. I didn't bother and pushed the button for the ground floor. I got off at the ground floor and went to MAC cosmetics store. I decided to buy some make up suited for my skin tone. I was greeted well by the lady at the store and she didn't show any signs of discomfort from me being at her store. She treated me just like she treats other customers.

Me: I need a concealer, foundation and face powder for my skin tone.

Lady: Which shade do you use ma'am?

Me: I am an amateur at makeup and all this while I have been using the wrong shade. This is the first time that I would be using a MAC product for makeup.

Lady: Don't worry, I will help you out.

She took out a few shades and selected NW51 to be the shade that would give me a natural look. They didn't have foundation for my skin tone in their stock.

I bought the concealer and face powder and left the store thanking the lady. The next stop was Pantaloons. It was on the ground floor as well, so I started walking to the other end of the mall. As I walked, a few looked at me, some gave me a shocked look but the majority of the people didn't bother! There were a handful of ladies who even smiled at me. I could read their eyes saying "Welcome to womanhood!".

I entered Pantaloons and went to the ethnic section where I checked out some beautiful skirts, kurtis and sarees. I selected a few skirts and placed them in the shopping basket. I then moved to the footwear section, where I looked for flats of size 41. When I couldn't find any footwear of my size, I turned to the western section. I avoided any interaction with the store executives as I didn't want to be in an unknown and uncomfortable situation. A store executive walked up to me.

Exec: Hello Ma'am, what are you looking for? Can I help you?

Me: I am looking for some jeans.

Exec: Ma'am what is your preference in jeans?

Me: Skin tight, high waist.

The executive showed me a few options and I selected the waist 28. Yes, I had a 28 waist that time. I wish I could go back from the present waist of 30 to 28 someday! I thanked the executive and got the items billed. Now I felt hungry and to have something, I had to climb two floors up to the food court. I took the escalators and reached the food court. On the way,

I didn't feel uncomfortable as I had gained some more confidence and even the walk came naturally now. I had a sumptuous dinner at one of the restaurants there and started my walk back to the parking lot. I felt content. I felt as if I had passed a test. It was a big day, another feather in the cap. Naina was growing up! I got into the car, kept the shopping bags on to the side seat and drove back to the hotel. I didn't change into Neel that night. I enjoyed some drinks in the hotel room with some music.

The Ambience Mall didn't judge me at all. In fact, it had accepted me with open arms and hugged me tight. I didn't care who laughed at me or who giggled at me. I didn't care if I made someone uncomfortable by sharing the space with them. I didn't care if someone was offended by my presence. The Mall accepted me and that was enough for me. It's my life and I was probably earning much more than 95 percent of the crowd at Ambience Mall. So, who were they to decide if I should be there or not. I was proud of who I was, and I had started to love myself.

CHAPTER FIFTEEN

GUDIYA

Born as a boy in an upper middle-class family, I showed feminine signs at an early age. It was the month of December 2014 and I had finally decided to open up to my parents. This is one thing that I would not be discussing much in this book. I think the dynamics and the drama deserve a separate book altogether. So, I was thrown out of the house for wanting to be a woman. Living two lives in one body had become a bit depressing. The process of transitioning into a woman was very satisfying but the reverse was depressing. In fact I felt humiliated, disgusted and cheated that I was born in the wrong body. I felt that I was a mistake and sometimes wanted to even kill myself.

I had quit my job before coming home to open up about my desire to transition into a woman. When I saw no positive response from home, I went back to NCR where I began winding up my luggage. I left the chunk of my luggage with the landlord and promised to take it soon. Dressed in a black salwar kurta with short hair and no makeup, I caught a train from Delhi to Ahmedabad where a man whom I had met on Facebook had invited me to come and stay over. All of a sudden, having no options I considered this to be a path shown by the almighty.

We had been in touch since July and it had been about five months now. I had even left my job as I wanted to concentrate on my transitioning and start my life afresh. I sold the car which was extremely dear to me. The train journey happened to be tricky as people were still trying to come terms with a transwoman travelling among them.

After reaching Ahmedabad, I tried calling this man and to my horror he just avoided my calls. Initially I thought that he may be busy with some work and may pick up my call eventually. I felt like a fool to have believed a total stranger just by his virtual touch! I felt disgusted, cheated and it seemed as if the end of the road was near for me.

Till the next morning I kept sitting on a bench at the railway station. It was not that I didn't have any money, but I didn't have the strength to face the world anymore. I had saved a lot of money in the past four years but had kept it all in a fixed deposit. I didn't sleep on the bench because I wanted to rest, but because I was too tired to even open my eyes.

In the morning, I felt a hand on my head from behind and someone said "Akeli kahan ja rahi hai gudiya", which meant "Where are you going alone, my doll?". She was Sapna, a eunuch hailing from the city of Bhuj. Once she heard my story and knew that I was well educated and didn't deserve to end up on the streets, she took me along with her to Bhuj.

I was a little skeptical in the beginning, but with no place to go to I hung in there. She took me to her home, a semi urban part of Bhuj where a whole group of around 6 transwomen stayed. She told me to be calm and not to worry. She narrated my story to others present there. They gave me a small room and said they respect my privacy, and I could stay there as long as I wanted.

I was happy at their home. I kept myself busy with household chores to make myself useful. In the meantime, I applied for jobs as well. A week had passed, and I decided to teach the ladies something and probably contribute to their upliftment. I started with teaching them English. They were initially very stubborn to learn, but since they had accepted me as their own, they had a soft corner for me.

I even used to go out with them all decked up in sarees for street food, which was my only option of outing there. They never asked me to go with them to weddings or railway stations for asking alms. After about 10 months, two ladies had learnt the alphabets and could recognize words written on boards. We still had a long way to go.

One day, when I was cooking in the evening, Zeenat came over, gave me a peck on my cheeks and handed over a gift-wrapped packet. I opened it to find a lovely saree in it. She said "Chal gudiya, aaj tujhe mandir le chalte hai" which means "Let me take you to a temple today, doll". Converted to Islam, she still visited temples. I asked her what the occasion was, but she just asked me to come. Draped in the lovely saree, I walked with them for around 3 kilometers to a small hillock where a temple was situated.

It was a small Hanuman temple where they had organized at pooja for my wellbeing. It was organized in a very colorful manner. As we entered the temple, Sapna didi pulled my pallu and covered my head. She gave me ten rupees note and a one-rupee coin. She then asked me to donate it at the temple. An old lady asking for alms was sitting over there. I just felt like giving a ten rupee note and touching her feet. I took out a ten rupee note from my blouse and gave it to the old lady. She blessed me and said looking at Sapna,

"Teri toli me ladkiyan kab se aane lagi", which meant "Since when did girls start joining your group?"

I told her "amma mai ladki nahi hu", which meant "Mother, I am not a girl"

She replied "meri aankhon me to tu ladki hi hai, khush reh aur hamesha hasti reh", which meant "You are a girl in my eyes, keep smiling forever".

Her words remain fresh in my ears. I can never forget her face and her blessings. I don't know where she is now or in wat condition. I just pray and hope that she is hale and hearty. She definitely has placed herself in a special corner of my heart.

I stayed with Sapna didi for another 4 months till I found a job in Delhi again in 2015. I still call up and keep up with what's happening with them. Had Sapna didi not met me that night, who knows I would have probably ended up at a brothel! I am still her gudiya and she keeps saying to me "meri gudiya naam kamaegi aur apni didi ka naam roshan karegi".

CHAPTER SIXTEEN

MY TRYST WITH GOA

I had never been to Goa until 2017 when I finally started my life as Naina. I had started my hormone replacement therapy and was done with my sittings with a few psychiatrists. I was starting to see some changes in my body, although these were very minimal and only, I could make out what changed and what didn't yet. A distant trip as the new me was pending as I had moved to a very serene place in Himachal Pradesh.

Living at a holiday destination didn't give me the urge to plan a getaway to any other place. I wanted to travel, meet new people and find myself. Travelling was something which has always remained close to my heart. Travelling, especially by road in my car or bike gave me so much insight to the varied cultures and traditions that we as Indians are proud of. The amalgamation of so many different kinds of people, style of living, languages and the variety of tea and food in different states excited me.

I called up Tanya, who stayed in Delhi, to ask if we could plan a trip to Goa. She was privy to the deep secrets in my life since the nascent years of Naina and was kind enough to have supported me emotionally. She agreed and we decided on a date. I asked another friend of mine who was a crossdresser, went by the name of Sonya. She was a friend of mine since the year 2013, whom I had met through social media. Sonya is a professional working in Gurgaon and is presently transitioning into a beautiful woman.

Sonya too agreed to tag along for the trip. Now I began searching for resorts in Goa that would be accommodating enough for a transwoman, a crossdresser and a cis woman to have some privacy and have a nice trip to remember. I emailed a few resorts at Agonda beach which lay towards the southern part of Goa.

I wanted to go to south Goa because of its serene beaches and being less commercialized, meant less crowd and lesser people to deal with during my holidays. I got a reply from Manveer's Kitchen which was located bang on the Agonda beach. The reply was very positive, and Manveer booked the rooms for us.

The next part was to decide where I was going to stay in Delhi, since I had a stopover. I looked for places on Airbnb which were recommended by a few friends. I received positive replies from many hosts. I chose to stay in a home maintained by a young couple who were happy to host me.

I booked my air tickets from Delhi to Goa and back. I chose to select the flights which ran late in the night, since I wanted to avoid active crowd at the airport. I was still not completely confident in presenting myself to the world.

I decided to meet Tanya and Sonya at the resort in Goa directly. Although there was an option of tagging along with one or both of them and go as a gang, I wanted to try and travel alone. I caught a bus at night from Nurpur, Himachal Pradesh for Delhi and reached early morning from where I caught an auto rickshaw and reached the Airbnb home. I was greeted with warmth and helped in settling down. The hosts were well educated and well to do. They kept ensuring that I was comfortable and left no stone unturned. I booked a cab for the airport to catch the flight to Goa. The flight was way past midnight.

I decided that it was time for me to start wearing jeans and shirts too. So, I decided to flaunt a maroon checkered shirt with sleeves folded to the elbows and a skin fit jeans. I paired it up with flats. My govt approved ID still showed me as a male and I was scared if that would be an issue at the airport. I had researched a lot online about this and also interacted with a few friends who had travelled by air post their transition.

I reached the airport, took a trolley, placed my suitcase and handbag on it and started walking towards the entry gate. I was asked by the security personnel to produce my ticket and ID. He glanced at my ticket and compared the name on the ticket from the ID. He then checked the photo on the ID and my face. He could make out that I was a transwoman and transitioning into a woman. He gave me back my ID and ticket as I was allowed to enter the airport. At the check in counter, the airline executive was warm with me and even upgraded my seat to somewhere in the front.

I proceeded for the security check. Here my only fear was whether I would be asked to join the men's line. I looked like a girl but there were traces of my male life which reflected to an extent on my face. Thankfully that didn't happen. The lady checked me inside the cabin and I was allowed to go ahead. I thanked her and she replied with a smile.

I spent my time in the smoking lounge and window shopping and was not bothered by people who wanted to decipher me! When someone walking by tried to stare at me for a longer time, I just stared back at them and then I was safe for a while! I did smile at a few women who looked at me with admiration and love. I used the ladies' restroom and no one had any problem with that. I was looked upon as a woman and I felt good.

I boarded the flight and we took off for Goa. It was a two hours plus flight and I kept myself busy munching and watching a movie on my mobile phone. I faced no problem from the fellow passengers and even the air crew was warm.

We landed at Goa, and I took a cab to the hotel nearby as my booking at Manveer's was starting next day. I slept peacefully. Sonya arrived at the hotel in the morning. She changed into her femme avatar and we set course to Manveer's Kitchen at Agonda.

Goa was beautiful! I cursed myself as to why I had never come to Goa. The people were so friendly and the place was so serene and clean, especially the south. Manveer's Kitchen was located bang on the beach and our rooms were facing the beach. Tanya was already at the resort as she had checked in early morning.

The watermelon juice felt so refreshing which I had ordered as soon as I reached. We checked into our rooms, which were small but practical and affordable. We sat at the restaurant in the evening where we befriended a Belgian lady who worked as a volunteer for an NGO which provided a home for the sick and stray animals in Goa. Her name was Brendy, who treated me and Sonya just like any other girls. Acceptance! I already felt good about this trip.

We enjoyed the evening celebrating Sonya's birthday too. I had ordered a bouquet of flowers and cake for her. We went back to our rooms and retired for the day.

The next morning, we hit the beach. I was dressed in a denim hot pants and a slim fit shirt. My breasts had started to grow but I still needed some amount of padding in my bra to fill the B cup. I was petite and I had worked a lot on my walk and mannerisms, which gave me a lot of credibility to be accepted as a woman by strangers. I still wore a wig since I hadn't grown my hair long enough, but I wasn't sad about it. My makeup had improved a lot and I could bring out decent looks with minimal make up too. We played in the water, walked on the sand and clicked photographs. In the evening, we explored both the sides of the beach and checked out other places for food and stay for the future. But, trust me, I always went back to Manveer's Kitchen!

Tanya and Sonya decided to explore the nearby Palolem beach for parties in the late evening. I didn't feel like going anywhere else and took an excuse to stay back. They left dressed in their short party clothes on a rented scooter, and I decided to go to the restaurant at the resort and have some beer.

I had recently started working as a content writer and was working on an assignment. I took my laptop to the restaurant and worked a little with some beer and food. I noticed a few couples around but what grabbed my attention were two girls probably in their early teens who were sitting at the corner table. They were staying in the room next to me and I had noticed them earlier too. They never failed to give me a smile when they passed by.

I finished my work and decided to move back to my room and enjoy beer outside my room which had some sitting space facing the beach. I put on some music and kept dancing to the tune. The two girls were going back to their room. I just started a conversation with them, expecting them to reply.

Me: Enjoying the Saturday night at the resort only? No plans for parties at Palolem?

First Girl: Hey! No, we just wanted a quiet evening. I am Sanya!

Second Girl: I am Niveditha.

Me: Hi, I am Naina. I hope the music won't be bothering you. If it does, then I can turn it off.

Sanya: No no, if you want you can join us, we are also sitting outside the room.

Me: That would be nice.

Sanya and Niveditha were students on a getaway from Pune. They were wonderful girls who talked to me all night and understood my life. I got two more friends for life. We have remained in touch since then.

Tanya and Sonya returned with a rented car which as occupied by three men. The men along with Tanya and Sonya reached where we were sitting. The men were interested in taking us to Karwar. I showed no interest and even asked Tanya not to go with them. The men finally left the place after exchanging phone numbers with Tanya. The next evening Sanya and Niveditha were to leave for Pune. We all spent time talking over lunch at the restaurant. We made new friends, shared experiences and made a small place in each other's hearts. As the trip was coming to an end, I felt sad. I wanted this to continue forever and never end, but holidays do come to an end. We thanked Manveer and left the resort. Manveer's wife Kavita and their son along with the pets that they had made our stay comfortable. We enjoyed thoroughly and made memories forever. Manveer and Kavita are like a family to me now. We keep texting each other occasionally.

CHAPTER SEVENTEEN

PAMPERED BY SALONS

By 2018, I had started experimenting a lot with my looks. My features were naturally sharp, still I lacked the art of accentuating them with the help of makeup. I had learnt about different products that went into makeup. I had learnt the difference between a foundation and a concealer, a kajal and an eyeliner, a lipstick and a lip liner and also got to know about highlighting. I loved eye makeup and lip coloring the most. I wanted my lips to look bigger and plump and wanted my eyes to give that depth.

Whenever I was in Delhi, I tried to reach out to make up artists and salons that could give me a makeover. These makeovers helped me understand the nuances of makeup and also different products that went into the process. I understood the sequence of application of various products which helped me in doing my own make up.

Most of the salons were friendly and only those which were located in semi urban areas refused to work on my face. For some, it was a taboo to do make up on a transwoman, for others it was an experience. It was not just me, but they also learnt something new while working on my face. I tried premium salons too but at a budget.

I started waxing my body and frankly speaking, I never felt it was painful! Threading my eyebrows had become a normal affair and facials were something that came with it. Pedicure and manicure had become my best friends and I was happy to have acquainted with them. My feet and palms were softer than ever before. Aloe vera gel and coconut oil were happy keeping the glow on my face intact. I took turmeric baths occasionally. My facial hair had almost gone, but I still needed some amount of shaving twice a week.

Visits to salons had become a monthly affair and it had become a place where I wasn't judged. I could ask for whatever service that I wanted. I just needed money in my bag, that's all! All my life I heard women talking about how they went to a salon and got a makeover or got a hair do or got their nails painted or got a pedicure.

Watching beauticians working on women during weddings in my family that I attended, I always felt jealous. I loved the fragrance that a woman carried back from a beauty parlor. I wanted to smell the same way. It felt so feminine and romantic! I was asked many a times by beauticians to grow my nails longer, but nails remain something which irritates me when they cross a certain length. So, I am still happy with temporary nail extensions whenever I need them. Talking about hair, I developed hair loss because of which I was forced to reduce their length and continue using wigs.

I moved to human hair wigs that I could glue on my scalp and remove after about fifteen days. It gave me the freedom of taking a bath with the wig on too. Compromises are fine till the time they don't hurt you badly and I was living as a woman already. I was content.

CHAPTER EIGHTEEN

FASHION ANXIETY

This chapter includes my feelings towards feminine clothing and how the perspective changed over a period as I grew up as Naina. I thought of including it, so that the people who are planning a journey similar to mine will get some idea about the thought that goes into selecting clothes. I always loved sarees and considered them to be the epitome of femininity.

A well-tailored blouse and a well draped saree can make anyone look pretty. This is what I thought. Although it is right to some extent, it is the attitude that a person carries which defines how well dressed they are. I chose only sarees till 2010 and even salwar kameez didn't make me feel feminine. I experimented with Anarkalis and salwar suits only until 2011. I was not comfortable with western outfits and always had a perception that my they wouldn't suit my body. I had a fear that I would look like a man in a women's clothing.

The attitude changed but it took its time. I went through a lot of trial and error methods to choose clothes that suited my body type. Born in a man's body, inspite of being petite, I had broader shoulders ad longer arms than women. My lower body was very feminine thanks to my thighs and buttocks which any woman would love to have! My feet were longer than women of my height and I was forced to use footwear of size 41 which were a rarity till recently, when a lot of fashion brands started focusing on taller women too.

Experimenting with salwar suits and western clothes was still fine, but wearing jeans with a shirt and still feel feminine was difficult for me till a certain time. It took a lot of effort and manifestation to graduate to a different wardrobe.

I realized that it was all attitude that mattered. How comfortable you were in the clothes and how confidently you could carry yourself in that look, is what mattered. I noticed that I was wearing the clothes for my happiness and if I looked pretty in the mirror to myself then, I didn't have to bother about what others thought about me or how I looked. I didn't ask for their opinion, right?

Sarees still have a special place in my heart and to this date I love buying sarees over any other attire, but that doesn't stop me from experimenting with other clothes too. I dress for an occasion depending upon what I need to do there. I have even draped a saree for a flight travel and didn't feel uncomfortable at all. On the other hand, once I was wearing a jumpsuit which resulted in a wardrobe malfunction at the airport restroom! Thankfully, I walked out of it unshaken!

Today, I love buying different types of trousers and pairing them up with tees and shirts. I have grown comfortable in flaunting a readymade crop top with a saree. I can do with a loose fitted salwar kurta too and still feel feminine enough. So, one needs to realize that it's all about how one thinks. Perception can set you back or make you sail ahead. The choice is yours and no one else gets to decide what you want to wear.

Today, I keep getting messages from crossdressers who are afraid to wear western clothes or think about any attire other than a saree. My message to them would be to keep experimenting. Some experiments go right while some go wrong. What matters is, what one has learnt from the mistakes. Even if it fails, at least one has an experience to remember!

CHAPTER NINETEEN

ENTERING THE GLITZ WORLD

Covid-19 struck the world in the year 2020 and everyone was confined to the four walls of their house for months. Work from home had become a norm and people started taking life more seriously. This continued till almost 2021, which affected travel too. I was sure lucky enough to have survived the pandemic in good health and even finances. One day while scrolling through my social media account, I came across an advertisement which read "Miss & Mrs. Saree Queen Season 1 – a virtual pageant from the comfort of your home. Apply now for a virtual audition". I saved this picture to my gallery.

The next day the same advertisement appeared again on my screen. Now, I was tempted to message the organizers "Glamour by Sara, Malaysia" to get more details and know if I being a transwoman could participate. To my surprise, Sara ma'am messaged me back confirming that I could take part in the Miss category and she would be happy to see me in the auditions.

My audition took place on Zoom call in the mid of August 2021. I was dressed in a beautiful saree for the auditions and believed to give my best. I was auditioned by Ms. Sara and Ms. Divyangana Mehta, both veterans in pageantry. I answered all their questions well and seemed confident.

I waited for the results that would be declared to announce the semifinalists for the pageant. Within three days, I got a message from Sara ma'am confirming me to be a semifinalist of Miss Saree Queen season one organized by Glamour by Sara, Malaysia. I was thrilled to have been selected among cis women at a pageant, although virtual, but it was a big achievement for me. I was added to a WhatsApp group which included all the 30 semifinalists. I made friends with Divya, Gunjan, Saloni, Shreya, Sunita, Megha, Priya, Yuga, Sonam, Kainaz, Sumitra, Dhanashree, Poonam, Nupur and a few more.

We went through a series of grooming and training sessions wherein we were taught about confidence, motivation, make up, cat walk and what not! We had a wonderful session by Ms. Shilpa Rao, who was our Vision Coach. Although I couldn't attend her session due to personal reasons, I learnt a lot from performing the task that she had assigned to us. We also had a session on cat walk by Ms. Sharwita, who was our Runway Coach. Ms. Seetu was our styling coach and her class was the most interesting class for me as she taught us three different ways of styling a saree which ignited a hunger in me to come up with different styles of draping a saree. All these sessions were on Zoom call, and it was fun interacting with all the ladies on the platform.

I developed a very close association with a few of them and we had mutual admiration for one another. I never felt, not being part of the women fraternity! I was accepted from day one into the pageant and the atmosphere was extremely friendly.

My aim of participating in the pageant was not to win. I didn't even hope to even clear the auditions. My aim was to gain experience and every task that I performed, I did it sincerely and put my heart and soul in it. I didn't shy away from asking questions regarding the tasks that we were given. I am sure I must have troubled Sara ma'am very much with my questions, but she always used to reply to me with an answer and solve my dilemma. As per Sara ma'am, I had performed really well in all the tasks and was selected for the Grand Finale.

One of the jury members were the famous SuTa sisters from the brand SuTa who were like idols to me! A month back, I had bought myself a saree from SuTa and had even performed a task wearing that saree! Their announcement as one part of the judges came as a pleasant surprise to me. I had missed out on the last few tasks due to some health condition that I was facing and I was even planning to withdraw from the pageant. Sara ma'am, Shilpa ma'am and Divya always stood by me and pushed me to finish the pageant. They were true angels for me during my times of crisis during the pageant.

When the Finale arrived, every finalist was to be asked a question by one of the judges and I prayed to the almighty to give me a chance to atleast speak to the SuTa sisters, even if I were not able to answer their question well. I was granted this wish and they asked me,

Sujata & Tanya: Hi Naina, what in your opinion is the most precious thing in the world?

I had about 30 seconds to answer this question.

Me: Hello ma'am, in my opinion, money and fame both can be earned but what remains precious is Time, which cannot be gained, once lost.

That's all I had as my answer. I later felt that I had given a very short answer and the judges may have expected a little more elaborate reply.

The pageant had come to an end, and I was awarded the First Runner Up of Miss Saree Queen and the sub title of "Miss Perseverance". I was ecstatic and my happiness touched the skies! However, I still feel that Divya deserved my crown much more than me, maybe it's the friend in me talking. Sara ma'am and Shilpa ma'am remained my mentors even after the pageant. I was sent a crown and a sash by post, with which I clicked a lot of pictures. Divya and the other girls are still in touch with me and at times the old WhatsApp group wakes up   from   hibernation!

CHAPTER TWENTY

MISS CONFIDENT

After being crowned the First Runner Up at Miss Saree Queen, I had been very active on social media and had been gaining a lot of followers organically. I was interacting with my followers on a regular basis and was happy about all the attention that I was getting. I was getting better at my styling and more confident in front of the camera. I was getting noticed!

I happened to see another advertisement on my social media account feed. It read "Miss Rainbow Pride of India 2022 organized by Hey Foundation". It was being organized at Mumbai in the month of March and coincided perfectly with the dates that I had planned to take a break from work. I auditioned for this pageant in the Miss category. I was selected for the Grand Finale and heart in heart I knew, I would.

Dr Sangeeta Patil was the brain behind this pageant who constantly works for the community. Her daughter Lavanya is a pageant winner, and she was also involved in organizing the event. I booked my tickets for the 10th of March to Mumbai and planned to attend the pageant on the 11th. I also planned to meet a lady named Archana Gupta, who had been treating me like her daughter since the time she had met me on Facebook.

I had started finding out more about the pageant through their page on Instagram and also pages from google search. I contacted Ruhaani and Jony, who were the last season's title holders. They were so friendly and accommodating in answering all my queries. It was as if we connected naturally. I never expected them to be so down to earth and friendly. They were definitely deserving candidates for the crowns that they were holding. I also saw the pictures of the other finalists on the pageant page. I was numb feet, as I felt they all looked prettier and more talented than me, but I was determined to give it my best shot.

I again had no aim of winning, but to enjoy the pageant and gain experience. There were two rounds which were to happen at the Grand Finale at Mumbai – Ethnic round and Western round. I chose to wear a black gown for the western round and a traditional kasavu saree for the ethnic round. Zainab, a Mumbai based designer helped me in realizing these outfits for me.

I took the flight to Mumbai on 10th and was received by Archana ma. She took me around the city and dropped me off at my hotel. I had chosen a hotel that was located close to the event's venue. Although, I wanted to spend more time with Archana ma, she insisted that I take rest before the pageant and showered me with blessings before she left.

I had contacted a beautiful singer who also did nail art as a hobby. We had become good friends and found a connection. She insisted that she would do my nails before the pageant. Kajal came to my hotel and did my nails beautifully. I also happened to meet a childhood friend of mine, Arushi, who was married and well settled in Mumbai. She had entered the world of motherhood recently and was glowing! I met her at a café, and we spent the evening talking about our lives. It was beautiful catching up with her. By night, I realized that my stomach had some issue. I had to go to the bathroom at least 10 times before the pageant the next morning. I even got late by half an hour from the reporting time of 8 AM.

I checked out of the hotel and caught an autorickshaw to the venue. I quickly dragged my suitcase and carried my bag into the venue where I met Beyonce, a gorgeous co-participant. She is one among the most popular drag performers in India now and is a very popular figure in the community. She was beautiful as well as immensely sweet and caring. I also happened to meet the organizers Sangeeta ma'am and Lavanya.

We had a choreo session where we were shown how we would enter the stage and leave. The correct method was taught to us and I was sure that I would end up making some mistake and make a fool of myself. I was getting a bit nervous seeing the other participants and that is when I reminded myself that I was there not to win the title but to win hearts and gain experience.

Post the choreo session, we went to the green room where we were supposed to get ready for the Ethnic round. I quickly draped my saree and began my make up. I left my hair open due to time constraints, later I felt I should have tied it up in a bun which I had planned for earlier. The Ethnic round started, and my entry number was eight. I could see Jony and Ruhi sitting in the audience. They were stars for me, not just because they were the title holders, but for the beautiful heart they had. I could see them smiling at me! I knew that my walk wasn't perfect, and I probably walked too fast. I gave a good crisp introduction and walked back.

The next round was the Western round and I changed into my evening gown. The gown had a slit which exposed one leg and heels very beautifully. I felt I had walked better in the western round. We were asked many questions by the jury, and I was lucky to have been selected in the final ten that included all categories.

I actually felt lucky, because the selection was based on voting from the audience and I knew no one in the audience except Ruhi, Jony and a judge Shivali. So, I wasn't expecting to stand amongst the last ten that included participants from three categories. Finally I was awarded a subtitle "Best Confidence" and I felt floating amongst the stars! I realized that I had started to walk and talk as "Miss Confidence" since quite some time, which helped me win this sub title. Confidence was something that has always been a propelling factor in my life, which was proved at this pageant.

The participants are still in touch with me and here too, I made friends for life. Sangeeta ma'am is also like a mother, who takes care of everyone as her own. She has been a kind supporter since the time I met her and constantly guides me in whatever way possible. Jony is like a soul sister now. She stays in Delhi, and I often meet her whenever I stop at Delhi.

CHAPTER TWENTY-ONE

A HOME AT DELHI

It was the year of 2019 and I was still in my getting along with my transition. I had made a lot of new friends, especially ladies through social media, a few of whom I was even able to meet in real life. Living as a woman wasn't easy especially when you had the tag of a transwoman coming with you. I even had to be careful about the places that I visited and also keep in mind the timings. I missed Delhi and wanted to go back to Delhi whenever given an opportunity.

My heart was truly in Delhi and the last trip that I had was way back in 2017 to Goa. It had been a long time since I had given myself a break. I used to take short breaks but stuck to places in and around Himachal Pradesh where I avoided crowd and enjoyed the serenity of the place.

A trip to Delhi was definitely on cards now and I even wanted to go clubbing. As Naina, I had almost given up on the things that I used to enjoy, like partying, clubbing, a hot cappuccino at a coffee shop or going all out on shopping from the malls!

Financially I was strong and never faced an issue. My fixed deposits were still intact and I was proud of the decision that I had made almost a decade back. I decided on the dates for my Delhi visit and looked for various options for the stay. I had avoided staying at hotels since the time I started living my life as Naina.

I had heard a lot about Hotel The Lalit, New Delhi from my friends about how supportive they were towards the LGBTQ+ community. Mr. Keshav Suri, a business magnate and the head of the Lalit Suri Hospitality Group, has always been upfront in fighting for equal rights for the community in India. His efforts have shown the path to thousands of people from the community, who had no future. The Keshav Suri Foundation, started by him, has given hope to many people from the community, whom I personally know. So, I decided to send an email to the reservations department of the hotel.

I found out the email address from their website and wrote a beautiful email, telling them who I was, my background and what I was looking for. I had mentioned specifically that this was going to be my first leisure trip as Naina to Delhi and what Delhi meant to me. I received a reply from Mr. Vivek Shukla who happens to be the Vice President, Operations, at the moment. I don't remember his appointment during those days. He assured me of a safe stay at The Lalit New Delhi and was delighted to host me. Soon, I even got a call from the reservations department and my booking was confirmed after taking into account my requirements.

I took a bus from Nurpur in night and reached Delhi by morning. I took a cab and headed straight to The Lalit which is located at Barakhamba Road, near Connaught Place. I was dressed in a crop top and jeans as I didn't want to look overdressed, moreover this was the most comfortable attire paired with a jacket for a journey from Himachal Pradesh.

The taxi reached the entrance of the hotel. I was greeted by the security guards present there. I was going to pick up my suitcase to place it on the conveyor belt at the security check when someone from the staff of the hotel picked it up and greeted me with a 'Namaskar'. I could already feel the positive vibes even before entering the hotel! The doors were opened for me as I entered the hotel. My luggage was tagged and a card was provided to me. I walked towards the reception.

Front Office: Namaskar ma'am!

Me: Namaskar, I have a reservation here by the name of Naina Menon.

Front Office: Yes ma'am, we have been eagerly waiting to welcome you. I hope you had a comfortable journey.

Me: Thank you so much, yes the journey was comfortable.

I read the name of the front office executive from his name tab. Anurag Chauhan, a very sweet guy, who always goes out of his way to help me out during my stay. He still works for Hotel The Lalit New Delhi and is a powerhouse when it comes to work.

Anurag: Ma'am, this is your room. You will be escorted to your room.

Me: Thank you so much Anurag.

I was greeted with a thali and a tika was applied to my forehead. I was given a bouquet of beautiful flowers at the front desk itself. I had to pinch myself to confirm that I wasn't watching a dream! I was then escorted to my room by a beautiful lady from the front desk. I don't remember her name now, as she had left the hotel before my next visit in 2020. We boarded the elevator and I was taken to the 21st floor of the hotel. We entered the room, which I found to be in a perfect state, readied up for me, keeping in mind my requirements! Now, who does this for a transwoman, whom no one knows! The lady asked me what I would prefer as my welcome drink, soon a glass of fresh watermelon juice arrived. She clicked a photograph of me and left. A few moments later, my luggage arrived, and it was placed on the luggage rack by the bell boy. He greeted me with a Namaskar! I meet him every time I am at Lalit. His name is Mr. Kewal and I lovingly call him "chacha"!

I dozed off for a while after opening up my luggage and putting them in the cupboard. I went to the restaurant which goes by the name of Al Fresco on the ground floor of the hotel, in the evening. I don't know how, but a word was put in to every department in the hotel about my stay and the whole staff was aware of how sensitive I was at that time of my transition. The manager at Al Fresco received me with so much respect and care. I had a strong coffee and read my book as the sun set. While I was going back to my room, someone came up and met me.

Unknown Man: Good Evening Miss. Menon, I hope you are having a comfortable stay.

Me: Yes of course! Thank you so much for asking!

I was informed about the various places that I could go to in the hotel and the services that I could avail. It was as if I had come home. Now someone would say that such a behavior is very common in luxury hotels. I would beg to differ! The Lalit group treats you very differently, maybe they went a step ahead to boost my confidence. They wanted me to go with the best memories and I definitely did!

I went back to my room and ordered the Lalit Signature Pizza. I spent the rest of the evening in my room itself. The next day I took an auto rickshaw and went to Connaught Place to shop for some cards that I wanted to leave for the staff before leaving the next day. I came back to my room and found that the housekeeping staff had left the room in the default state already! You would say, that's what happens everywhere, but you don't find a personal touch and love everywhere, do you?

I attended the party at Kitty Su, their club on the ground floor on the last night of my stay. I had bought a beautiful sea blue velvet gown for this party. It was probably the first evening gown that I had bought for myself in years! It was a sleeveless gown and I had grown over the inhibition of flaunting sleeveless attires! I paired it up with light make up and open hair. I decided to wear my flats since I didn't want to look too tall! The party was great, I met my friend Sonya here after two years and also made a few friends who still remain in touch.

The trip came to an end the next day and I packed the my luggage along with the box of chocolates that was kept in my room as a gift. I left handwritten cards as a token of appreciation for Mr. Vivek Shukla and his staff.

I am a regular visitor at this hotel and they have become more like a family to me now. I was lucky to have been invited by Mr. Akshay Tyagi who heads the branch Diversity, Equity and Inclusion at The Lalit Suri Hospitality Group, to the Pride Month Celebrations in July 2022. I was requested to even speak about my journey in front of a vibrant audience. The staff of the hotel remains very close to my heart. I cannot shy away from mentioning a few names of people who have always welcomed me at the hotel and made it a point to meet me whenever possible. Tonmoy, Mohul, Anusha, Vijender, Kewal, Shivangi, Sameer, Amrit from Kitty Su, Shaktiman, Devanshu, Anurag, Asif, Sangeeta, Victoria, Sibi, Satya, Bhishek, Ashish who heads the Front Office and Suraj and above all Mr. Vivek Shukla, who have been supporting me throughout the journey since the time I visited the hotel. I thank these wonderful human beings from the bottom of my heart and a huge ball of love for Mr. Keshav Suri who has trained a wonderful team who are not just professionals but good human beings too, which is a rarity in these times! I would forever remain indebted to them.

CHAPTER TWENTY-TWO

A PURE HEART

This incident happened sometime in the year 2019 when I had started taking hormones. I had started staying at a small town named Nurpur which happens to be the foothills unlike the hill station that you perceive Himachal Pradesh to be.

I had begun going out more often unlike the times when I used to restrict myself within the four walls of the rented house fearing social rejection! I was coming back from the supermarket after buying my fortnightly home supplies.

The streets were flooded with kids and the way the kids are, I was scared of anyone of them would raise fingers at me for being stuck as neither a man nor a woman. I started walking quicker as I had the last 500 meters stretch to my house. I wondered if I should have covered my head with the dupatta of my patiala suit.

I wondered if I should have tied up my hair into a bun or maybe a braid rather than leaving it open. I wondered if I should have dressed up in a tee and jeans. I wondered if my makeup was peeling off. So many questions pondered my head with permutations and combinations that only Einstein or Newton could solve.

Alas, the last hundred meters and I could see the passage onto the left side of the street leading to my house. As I was about to take that turn, a little girl of around 9 years of age started staring at me and said, 'Naina di, aap to aaj ekdum Tabu lag rahe ho'

I was surprised that she knew my name! This brought a wide smile on my face and I touched this girl's head saying 'God bless you'. She happened to be my neighbor's daughter(coincidentally named Naina) and still keeps calling me Tabu, though I find no resemblance with Tabu.

I later became her part time English tuition teacher too! I realized that kids see only the best in you and even if they see something bad, they blurt out immediately without even thinking! They are so pure and   full   of   goodness.

CHAPTER TWENTY-THREE

OPENING UP TO TANYA

Let's roll back to the year 2013 when I was in Delhi for a year when the work from home concept was a bit new to all of us. I was granted the opportunity to work far from my company and it gave me a lot of freedom in terms of my time, which kept me sane!

My home party time mostly included draping a beautiful saree, putting on some make up, attaching a wig and spending time with some beer, snacks and dim lights! It also included occasional cooking and doing household chores which kept me healthy and the house spic and span.

After months of regularly doing this, I was a little bored and Naina really wanted to grow more. I decided that I should tell my bestie Tanya about this. She also stayed in Delhi, and we met almost every weekend. So I called her up and I was somehow able to tell her this.

Tanya - Are you pulling my leg or something?

Me - no... Do u want proof?

Tanya - show me your pictures.

I sent her a few pics and as soon as she saw them, I deleted them! She called me back.

Tanya - Dude, u look hot! I wish I had a body like yours! You have naturally femme features! We could hit the bar this weekend and I am sure so many guys would hit on you!

Me - Tanya, stop kidding!

Tanya - I am serious babe, let's meet up this weekend. Let's do this.

Though we didn't go to a pub the coming weekend, we decided to go to a lounge in Gurgaon. We checked into a hotel at Mahipalpur and told the reception that I had to get ready for a stage performance at Gurgaon.

The receptionist was kind enough and after an hour he saw me in a beige yellow saree coupled with a full-sleeved black net blouse! He couldn't recognize me initially due to the makeup and the wig but could make out later. He gave me a weird smirk, I ignored. Tanya was with me and that was a source of strength for me. We took a cab. In the cab -

Tanya - Sweety u look beautiful!

Me - *blushing*

Tanya - what do I call you???

I didn't call myself Naina at that time. I changed my name three times since then and settled for Naina in the year 2017.

Tanya - call me Veronica!
(I don't know why I chose that name!)

Tanya - ooh la la... The sexy Veronica!

So, this was my first outing with a friend as the real me. We went to the lounge and no one bothered to even ask me why I was dressed in a saree. Figure wise I could have given any young girl a run for her money but face wise, I was yet to learn the nuances of makeup. Natural femme features helped me sustain myself as a woman to an extent in the public, although second looks were assured!

On the way back to the hotel, I felt like I had achieved something big. It was as if I had reached a new high in my life. I started to think, why did I enjoy much more than my regular outings? Am I just a crossdresser or a transwoman? The questions kept pondering my head, but I was so happy that they didn't burden me. This was a big day for me.

Tanya - goodbye my sassy girl! Stop blushing!

Me - You were really fine with all this?

Tanya - how does it matter if you are a man or a woman. Even if you decide to live your life as a woman one day, I am there for u girl. For me what matters is that you are my friend, and your happiness is important. It doesn't matter how you lead your life till the time you aren't hurting anyone. So, my love, start taking care of your skin and I want this saree of yours, I will get you my short black dress for you that you admired last week! Mwah. Bye.

I went back to the hotel, changed, checked out and went back to my house. I suddenly felt that all the happiness had evaporated. This was the start to something big in my life.

CHAPTER TWENTY-FOUR

THE SURGERY

At the end of the year 2021, just before COVID-19 hit the world, I managed to step further into the world of femininity. I had been planning to undergo breast augmentation surgery to enhance my breasts. Breast augmentation is a cosmetic procedure to increase the breast size. The hormone supplements that I was taking had been effective only to a certain extent in enhancing my breasts.

I had saved enough money for breast augmentation and even my sex reassignment surgery. I decided to go for my breast augmentation surgery in Delhi after a lot of thought. I decided not to go through the sex reassignment surgery at that moment. Sex reassignment surgery or gender reaffirming surgery is a surgical procedure by which a transgender or non-binary person's appearance and/or sexual characteristics are altered to resemble those associated with their identified gender and alleviate gender dysphoria.

I contacted a hospital in Delhi and went for an appointment. I met the doctor who was assigned to me and he took a note of my requirements. I wanted to start experiencing the feeling of having breasts while still looking natural, in accordance with my height, weight and build. I didn't want to exceed a B cup. I was already wearing a 36 B cup, but always filled them up with silicon pads to make them look fuller. These silicon pads made survival in peak summers extremely difficult due to sweat and heat. I always used to end up adjusting my bra several times and even had to go to washroom to readjust the pads.

The doctor examined my breasts and also showed me on his computer how my breast would look like post the surgery. The pre operative examination included assessment of my breast mound, nipple position and evaluation of the shape and size of my breasts. My posture was also evaluated. I kept looking at the image and wondered if I would really have those breasts soon! I felt that, after the surgery, even my bra would say, "Now don't you dare accumulate fat anymore, there is no space left for us!"

I was asked to stop smoking for some time and eat good nutritious food. I don't want to get into the details of how the surgery was conducted, because I have always been scared of needles and hospital procedures and makes me uncomfortable, even writing about it. The surgery left me with stitches. The first two days post the surgery were immensely painful. I was given strong doses of painkillers that helped me survive through that phase. I had to wear a compression bra for about two weeks, that helped in the healing process.

The mirror showed me beautiful breasts, that I had imagined only in my dreams. My breasts felt numb for some days, but I was fine in due course. I was advised to do some exercises to reduce the firmness of the breasts by the doctor. I felt so beautiful from inside after having these breasts.

I felt like my body was growing beautiful day by day. The major reason was changing my thinking. I felt beautiful from inside and every single day, I made it a point to thank the Almighty for this life and for making me beautiful. I noticed a lot of changes in my skin, posture and features.

CHAPTER TWENTY-FIVE

A SUPERWOMAN

It was the year 2013 or 2014 and I had already been going out secretly dressed up as a woman in Delhi though I still lived the life of a woman trapped inside a man's body. It was the end of September and the summers were on the verge of winding up. I had joined a group on FB which kept giving me information about the queer parties happening in Delhi. I had heard about a lot of parties happening in and around CP for our community. I had never attended such a party at CP and was thinking of doing it soon. I had come across the invitation on the group for an LGBTQ+ party at a pub in Delhi.

I finally decided that it was time to attend this on a weekend! I went to the Ambience Mall Gurgaon and started checking out some gowns. There was one store which had beautiful gowns. One black gown caught my eye since it was made from my favourite fabric - velvet! It was the perfect gown for me since it had a beautiful back cut and sleeves touching my elbow. I bought it without looking at the price tag.

I went back to my room and quickly started my beauty regime. I took a hot shower, shaved(hurts), put on a face pack and painted my nails. I got into my essential lingerie and slipped on the black velvet dress. I took out my 5 inch heels from the wardrobe and wore them. I then did my make up and put on my wig. I was all set! I looked in the mirror and I saw Veronica! I blushed and giggled with happiness!

I called for a taxi. There was this man who drove an Uber whom I had met during one of my outings. I had never ever found a better man than him driving a taxi! He took care of me like a big brother. He took me wherever I wanted to go and waited till I came back to drop me home. He never charged me more than the actuals. More about him in some other story. So he called me up confirming his arrival at the gate of my building. I switched off my corridor lights, took my purse and sneaked out of the house ensuring that my neighbors didn't get a hint!

I removed the heels and instead of taking the lift, I walked down five floors of my building. I took the way less taken and reached the cab. I guided bhaiya to the location. I was nervous as I had to walk the last distance from the taxi to the mall alone where the pub was located. I walked a few steps with fear and suddenly courage hit me. I started swaying my hips and walked as if I was the prettiest girl on earth, with so much confidence that I felt pretty from inside!

I reached the pub safely and at the entry a few men stared at me, a few bad eyes and the rest didn't bother. I entered and found the lights to be dim, like really dim that I could hardly make out any faces. I found a corner seat and settled with a drink. I found guys trying to start a conversation with me a few times but most of them were the "FRANDSHIP types", totally a turn off!

So, I was happy sitting alone. I went to the floor after a while and started dancing alone enjoying the music. I felt a hand rubbing against my buttocks. I thought it may have been by mistake since it was getting crowded. I felt the same thing again and I looked at this guy and walked away to the bar. I felt disgusted and asked for another drink.

I saw another transwoman standing by my side, she is still one of the prettiest transwomen that I have ever come across! So that guy tried to do the same with the transwoman standing by my side. The next thing that I saw was this guy flying about ten meters and sliding the next ten! The girl by my side kicked him on his buttocks and warned him not to do this to anyone. Wow! She was like a Wonder Woman! I happened to get in touch with her years later when I started transitioning. It so happened that her name was Veronika, with a K and not C which I used.

She lives somewhere in Mumbai and is a successful makeup artist. I give credit to her for giving me the strength to reply to men who don't behave! This was the page dedicated to all the women who know how to reply! She turned out to be a superwoman that evening for me and I admire the way she replied to the man in the only language that he would understand. That was when I met superwoman   Veronika!

CHAPTER TWENTY-SIX

KANHA'S RADHA

Who doesn't dream of dolling up in a pretty lehenga or a wedding attire and pump up the look with some jewelry and make up! Who doesn't dream of being a beautiful bride and steal all the attention for that single day. Who doesn't???

Let's go back to the year 2019 when life was a little better as Naina had realized a life out in the open. It was the winters and life was sailing and crawling at the same time. Sailing because I had found my purpose and crawling because of the hiccups which came from being a part of the society and trying to not follow its norms. I had happened to see the photos of a friend of mine who had just got married. Her Instagram post boasted of the gorgeous lehenga that she wore. Her jewelry was immaculate and the makeup made her look like a queen! Everyone around her in the pic was happy. She had found the love of her life. She had never looked that happy in her previous pics even when she wore pretty dresses.

I didn't feel jealous at all, I never do! But I felt an urge to be a bride! Be a bride for a day! Pamper myself and wear a beautiful lehenga, do some make up, wear nice jewelry and just chill! This sounded like a plan.

Why not be a bride for a day, for who knows I may not be able to be one ever! Why do I need a partner, an audience and a stage to be a bride. My groom could be Kanha. Why not! He is my eternal groom and will always look after me and give me the strength to look after myself! So, I picked up a lehenga that I had gotten made a few years back. It was a red and white lehenga with a red velvet choli of short sleeves and a red dupatta. It wasn't new since I had worn it a few times but never like a bride!

Sometimes I felt that it was a loud color and type and never really tried wearing it out. I dressed myself in this lehenga, did some make up with some extra pinch of eye makeup and to top it all, some jewelry that was in my almirah lying unused since a long time. I did my hair into a nice bun with a puff in the front. I put on a maang tika and nath and to complete the look I added a loud payal to my ankles!

I walked towards the mirror with the sound of the anklets cheering and applauding for me. The lights were the audience and they clicked my photos. The walls were my well wishers who blessed me. The mirror had arrived and it witnessed a beautiful bride who was the happiest woman on earth that day!

I clicked some pics that day and would love to share if lehenga pics can be shared in the comments section.

CHAPTER TWENTY-SEVEN

A MAN FROM THE PAST

It was the time when I had let out Naina completely and was living a respectable life as a full-time freelance content/ghost writer. This was the year 2021 and I happened to be invited to a friend's wedding at Delhi. The date coincided with my planned vacation and after a lot of self-persuasion I finally decided to attend the wedding. It was after a really long time that I was going to attend a wedding of someone known to me. My friend had promised me that the crowd would accept me and somehow she was sure that no one would know, thanks to the covid masks!

The drive from my hotel to the wedding lawn wasn't easy as a lot of things kept lingering in my head. Whom would I talk to, won't I get bored? My friend would be busy, it's her big day, where would I sit? What if someone feels uncomfortable being around me? What if it becomes embarrassing? I just shut my brain which was running at the speed of light and asked it to just go blank! I took out a cigarette (I know it's a bad habit, please don't judge me) and lit it in the cab.

As I puffed out the first smoke, I felt relieved and my head actually went blank. After finishing the smoke, I checked my makeup and sprayed my favourite Tommy Hilfiger perfume to negate the smell of the cigarette. We reached the destination. I quickly put on my mask, adjusted my saree and went in with a gift in one hand and my handbag in the other. I felt a little sweaty in my underarms even in the month of January!

I reached the mandap where the pheras were scheduled. My friend saw me and sent out a wide smile with a loud Hiiiii! We hugged each other and she asked me to stand behind her. I felt the acceptance was genuine from the people present and since only close friends and family had come, most of them had taken off their masks. I was still comfortable wearing the uncomfortable mask! The Pooja started and I was looking at my friend who was nothing less than an angel! I looked up and noticed a man smiling at me. It was a decent smile, probably the ones that affirm respect. He walked across, came and stood by my side.

This was a gentleman around 6 ft tall, handsome, gelled hair and trimmed beard look. He was dressed in a proper black suit and looked nothing less than a man from the Reid & Taylor ad! Oh wait, I know this man! Flashback into 2014, he was the man who worked in the same company! He was my senior and had trained me for six months before I was appointed to the post of Quality Analyst- Tester at one of the MNCs.

He - Good evening, ma'am! Such a pleasure meeting you after a long time!

Me - Hello sir, I didn't know you would remember me.

He - how can I forget my best QA Tester. The company misses you, so do I! We had a position for you in LA when you decided to quit. Moreover, Shikha had told me that you would be coming to the wedding and that's how I recognized you. You always had beautiful features!

Me - That is so sweet of you sir! Thank you so much.

He - I am not your sir anymore...(giving his hand for a handshake) Jai would be just fine!

Me - (shaking hands n blushing)

So I found company in a handsome man who was probably the center of attraction after the bride and groom. (Don't have your brains running about a love story here). We danced, had dinner, talked about our lives.

Me - You haven't changed a bit! You are still the same!

Hc - Sorry lady I can't say the same about you, because you have brought out your inner beauty!

He was his charming self the whole evening and he was gentleman enough to drop me back to my hotel room. I had no lovey dovey feelings for this guy and I am sure even he didn't for me. It was just when two people met from the past and celebrated the memories and created new ones as friends. My gender was finally sorted out, but my sexuality remained a question. He did hug me, gave me a peck on my palm but never ever made any advancements taking me for granted. What a gentleman! At no point of time I felt attracted to him romantically, as I had no attraction towards men. Even after having breast implants, I looked at men with expectations of being good friends. Being a friend to a man was also difficult for me, since childhood, I always felt out of place during the usual boy discussions. The only thing that I used to do with the boys was to play cricket and that I did till State Level, proving my worth.

Me - thanks Jai, it was wonderful catching up.

He - pleasure is all mine. I totally enjoyed your company. I am moving to LA next week. We still have an offer for you, and we would love to have your expertise at our LA office. If you say yes, we can get the formalities done in a few days at Hyderabad office.

Me - I don't know, I am happy with what I am doing at the moment and being out of QA Tester shoes for more than half a decade, I don't know if I would be able to do justice.

He - I totally understand Naina. Any assistance you need from me in the future, do let me know. Keep in touch.

Me - Didn't you feel awkward being with a transwoman?

He - You are a woman to me. I know the human in you and that human is better than anyone that I know in my circle! So, throw these ideas out of your head. You were, are and will always remain a wonderful human being and a friend. Oh, and for me you are like someone having the brains of Sushmita Sen, attitude of Nora Fatehi and elegance (don't remember He said elegance or looks or something else) of Kiara Advani.

Me - I can call you a liar for the last part.
(Hugged him and kissed him on the cheeks as we bid goodbye)

I couldn't meet him after that as I was to leave Delhi the next morning and presently he is in LA. We keep talking, chatting and video call frequently. It's nice to have such people in your life who come unexpectedly out of nowhere and make you realize that life is good! There is so much to cherish and celebrate. You never know what life holds for you in the future, so it is always important to live your life on your own terms, one day at a time.

CHAPTER TWENTY-EIGHT

REKHA MA'AM

Neel was a girl in the guise of a boy, all thanks to the wonders of the Almighty! She had short hair and was dressed in the binary clothes defined for a boy. The science class had just gotten over, and her wait was over as it was finally the class of her favourite teacher Miss Rekha Ajay. Rekha ma'am taught English to class 7 students and Neel aka Naina found Rekha ma'am to be stunningly pretty and mesmerizing as if whatever she said was sermon to Neel. Neel was a good student and was among the favorites of Rekha ma'am. Neel used to admire the beautiful sarees and salwar suits that ma'am used to wear.

I wondered if I could ever be like Rekha ma'am someday. Fast forwarding to 20 years, Neel was now Naina! I had lost touch with Rekha ma'am. I made all efforts to find contacts of Rekha ma'am. She couldn't be found on social media too. One day I googled her name along with her credentials and educational background and could locate a lady with similar name teaching at a school in Gurgaon. I immediately contacted the school and requested if they could inform Rekha ma'am about Naina, a long-lost student of hers! After a gap of two days, Rekha ma'am called me up and she instantly recognized this long lost student of hers! Rekha ma'am invited Naina to her home for lunch. I bought a carefully selected Kerala saree for my beloved teacher whom I looked up to all my life. When I gifted the saree to ma'am, she said.

'Beta, what was the need for all this.'

Naina replied, 'a mother shouldn't refuse a gift from a daughter'.

The reunion was a blessing, uniting two souls who had no relation of blood but maybe a past life relation. I realized that I looked so much like what ma'am looked back in those days! After hours of gossip and catching up, it was finally time to leave and as I touched my teacher's feet for blessings, she handed over a beautiful green Gadwali shawl to me.

Me: 'Ma'am why this formality!'

Ma'am: My daughter has come home, how can I send her empty handed.

I looked at my teacher's two sons, both admiring me like the elder sister that they never had! Abu and Adi are the only brothers that I have.

Some relations are made in heaven, and some are made by us during our lifetime which sometimes touch us more than blood relations.

AFTERWORD

Writing this book took a lot of time. I started writing this book in the year 2018 and after compiling a few events in my life into chapters, I lost my way. I had shared a few chapters with my friends to know how they felt about the idea of me writing a book about my life. I was compelled by many of my friends to continue writing the book as they felt my story needed to be told.

Initially I had thought of writing the book in a sequence, following a timeline, but I thought cascading my stories would be more fun to read. So, I kept compiling my stories as and when something reminded me of them. Still, the time period from 2020 to 2022 saw no addition to the book. It was only in the start of 2023 that I went full throttle with the book, when my mother Mrs. Rekha Ajay and Gurpreet Didi compelled me to finish the book. Gurpreet Didi used to remind me once every four-five months that the book was waiting to be made.

This book misses out on many people who remain close to me and play a very important part in my life. I didn't want this book to stretch on and will include the missed out people and events in my next book if I decide on writing it. My main intention of writing this book was to reach out to thousands of people like me, who were born in the wrong body, to give them hope and courage.

My message to you all would be to first get a good education, add as many skills as possible and build your capabilities. Education is the only thing that will help you when you have no support. It will give you a source of good employment and make you independent. These days, there are many companies that support our community and don't judge their employees on the basis of caste, creed, color or gender!

The world will accept us, but first we need to accept ourselves. I keep getting messages on my social media asking me – where, how, when etc. about various problems. Problems will not end if you seek them, one has to face them and try to solve them on their own. I never depended on anyone. I feel that, the problems and the struggles that I faced in my life are responsible for making me a strong woman today. I would have been nothing, had I not faced and come out of those problems on my own. I consider myself lucky that I was provided with a good education, because of which I never had to beg.

My message to people not belonging to the LGBTQ+ community is that, we too are human beings and deserve not to be judged by our choice of clothing, gender, expression or sexual orientation. Befriend someone from the community and try to understand us. We don't need sympathy; acceptance is just enough! I hope we can build a better world together and leave behind an environment that doesn't judge people, for our future generations where no one would have to live in fear of facing their real self to the world!

THE END